Captain John James Crowe V.C.

The Military
Exploits of
Captain John
James Crowe
V.C.

Doreen Pannett and Robin Pannett

Reveille
PRESS

Reveille Press is an imprint of
Tommies Guides Military Booksellers & Publishers

Gemini House
136-140 Old Shoreham Road
Brighton
BN3 7BD

www.tommiesguides.co.uk

First published in Great Britain by
Reveille Press 2013

For more information please visit
www.reveillepress.com

A catalogue record for this book is available from the
British Library.

ISBN 978-1-908336-62-0

Printed and bound by
CPI Group (UK) Ltd, Croydon, CR0 4YY

Contents

Introduction

WHEN MY husband Robin retired in the early 1990's we joined the Malmesbury Family History Society in Wiltshire. It was at this time he decided to research and write a book about my grandfather, Captain John James Crowe.

We began our quest with family. We knew we had relatives living in the Reading area whom we had never met and two of my mother's cousins, Don and Charles replied to our letters of enquiry and we arranged a Crowe family get-together at our house in Grittleton near Chippenham. My sister Andrea and her husband Colin came along with Fred and Hilda, Pat and our daughter Angela who was accompanied by her husband Nick. Photographs were shared amidst lots of conversation.

Our research then led us all over England after this initial meeting. Robin and I had a holiday in Ely where we visited the birthplace of J.J. Crowe's father in nearby March. Here we had an interesting visit to the local library as part of our investigations. Another memorable holiday was to Ireland where we visited Baltinglass and Saunders Grove – we saw the cottage where the Crowe family lived and were privileged to meet the current owner of Saunders Grove; being shown round some of the rooms. We also visited the church in Baltinglass where we were shown the baptism records of my Grandfather's brothers and sisters. Further visits were made to Bristol, London and Brighton following the trail of John James.

Robin sadly passed away in 2004 before finishing this project and the research stopped, however, after the unveiling of a plaque to commemorate the battle of Neuve Eglise and the memory of Captain John James Crowe I decided to pick up where we had halted. This book completes this work.

Special thanks to Billy Hollis, Sam Eedle and Major John Cotterill for their assistance in commemorating John James, and in their support in completing this book.

The Crowe family are very proud of their relative. Captain John James Crowe V.C.

Doreen Pannet (Granddaughter of Captain Crowe)
2013

Chapter One

John's parents and his early family life

JOHN CROW, father of John James, was born on 16th may 1844 in March, Cambridgeshire. He was the second child born to James and Sarah Crow, a family that heralded from the fenlands of East Anglia. In 1848, the family moved to Sarah's hometown of Whittlesey, a place dear to their hearts. John and Sarah had been married there and it was also home to all four of John's grandparents.

At the time, the fenlands we know today were not yet completed and the Whittlesey Mere, although shallow, still existed. Similar in size to Lake Derwent, the Mere gave the area its distinctive character, covering more than 3,000 acres in winter. The lake was a popular spot in the summer months and accordingly stalls, sideshows, amusements and fairgrounds lined the shores. The area was alive with the hustle-bustle of Victorian England, no doubt it was a place frequented by John as a young boy.

Despite the pleasures of Whittlesey, John and Sarah moved to Boston, Lincolnshire, in 1853. By now, the young couple had a family of five. They were Harriet, John, Susan, James and Mary. Four more children were born in Boston, they were William, Robert, Sarah and Henry. Before long, however, the call of home proved too great so they returned to Whittlesey, where Matilda and Charles were born.

John did not come from an army background, indeed both his father and grandfather were vermin destroyers, a trade that was in high demand at the time. Evidently, this life was not for John, as on 6th February 1861, at the tender age of sixteen, he enrolled in the Royal South Lincoln Regiment of Militia. The army life must have appealed to John, as just after his nineteenth birthday he decided to make it his fulltime career. At a quarter to four in the afternoon on 21st May 1863, John took the Oath of Allegiance at Westminster Police Court, signing up for ten years as a member of the 104th Regiment South Lincoln of Foot. A copy of John's enlistment papers still exists and in which he is described as being 5ft 7ins tall with a chest measurement of 34ins, having grey eyes and brown hair. Receiving the Regimental Number 3255, he was soon sent to Parkhurst on the Isle of White. However, John's early days in the 104th were not without controversy. At the time, serving in a militia and in the regular army were not compatible career paths and as John had failed to declare his membership of the Royal South Lincoln Regiment of Militia, he was charged under the provisions of the Mutiny Act. This, in turn, resulted in him being sentenced to a loss of pay and service. Thankfully, John was forgiven for his oversight and the status quo was quickly resumed.

A little more than a year after enlisting, John left the shores of England, on 6th July 1864, bound for India, a place where he would serve for more than 11 years. The Suez Canal, a place we now take for granted, had yet to be opened and as a result John's voyage to India took over three months and involved the hazardous trip around the Cape of Good Hope – an experience which must have been terrifying for a young man from East Anglia.

Despite the dangers and the arduous voyage, John arrived safely in Calcutta on 15th October and set out for Jhansi. Over the next four years he would see much of the Sub-Continent, spending time in Sippiee, Morar and Dugashaie. By 1868, John had been posted to Peshawar and apart from a few months spent at Cholera Camp, he would spend the next two years stationed there. John's surviving army records are rather vague with regard to his two years at Peshawar but years later he recounted to his grandson Jack (the son of John James) stories about visiting the Khyber Pass, Jalalabad and Kabal. Despite the fact that the distance from Peshawar to Kabal is about 150 miles, it is quite possible that John visited these places. It was only some eleven years since the mutiny of 1857 and as a result, the British Army would have ensured that its presence was felt across the region, something that would have involved regular excursions and patrols.

In 1870, John was posted to Nowshera and Fort Attack, but by July 1871 he found himself stationed at Allahabad. John had clearly taken to military life as on 17th April he had extended his terms of service, signing up for a total of 21 years in the army. John's decision to extend his army career led to him transferring in August 1871 to the 36th Foot Regiment, receiving the new Regimental Number 1918. By November he found himself stationed at Rawalpindi, a place he was to stay until March 1873. His regiment would return to England in 1875 but before John returned home he spent time at several other places including Meen Mere, Dugshaie and Solace.

On John's return to England his regiment was based at Raglan Barracks, Devonport, near Plymouth, and it was here that he met Caroline Elizabeth Turpin, a twenty-two year old local girl. The two soon fell in love and were married at Stoke Dameral Registry Office on 20th October 1876. Caroline came from a large family and was the third child from six. Her siblings, as well as her parents, had all been born in Devonport and for many years they had resided on Cherry Garden Street in Devonport. However, not long after John and Caroline were married they moved to 2 Market Lane, Stoke Dameral.

Caroline Crowe. John Crowe's mother.

Captain John Crowe's father, John Crowe, in later years.

On 28th December 1876, Caroline gave birth to John James Crow at the Female Garrison Hospital in Raglan Barracks. Unfortunately, we know little concerning John James' early life. Indeed, due to the scarcity of records and the omission of Caroline and John James from the 1881 census, it can only be assumed that they were living in married quarters. We know more about the whereabouts of John Crow who, still attached to the 36th Foot, went to Pembroke Docks, Wales in November 1877 and then on to Fleetwood, Lancashire in March of the following year.

In February 1880, John transferred again, this time to the 48th Foot Regiment, at the time part of the 29th Brigade. During this time he again travelled to India, although on this occasion only for a few months. By the end of 1880, John found himself serving in Ireland, initially based at Tralee and then in 1881 at Tipperary. On 1st July 1881, after little more than a year with the 48th Foot, John transferred again, this time to the 1st Battalion Northamptonshire Regiment. He would remain with his regiment until he retired from the army in June 1884, spending the remainder of his career at Curragh Camp, near Dublin. It was here that John and Caroline had their second child on 22nd May 1883, Charles Frederick, although he was better known as Frederick.

By this time, John had served 21 years in the British Army and had been awarded the Good Conduct Medal and a gratuity. While in Her Majesty's service John had earned the basic pay of one shilling a day. In February 1869, he had also been granted good conduct pay, which amounted to an additional sum of one penny per day. This award was progressively increased

Grove House, Saunders Grove near Baltinglass, County Wicklow.

Grove Cottage, Where John crow and his family lived between 1885 and 1904.

until May 1881, when the amount reached five pence per day; the maximum payable for good conduct, meaning that John's family would have a secure future.

However, John's time in the army benefitted his family in other ways, too. During his service he had become an excellent rifleman and a crack shot, something that lead one of his commanding officers, Colonel Saunders, to offer him a job as a gamekeeper at his country estate. John readily accepted the position and he and his family would spend the next twenty years living at Saunders Grove, a 200-acre estate near to the market town of Baltinglass, County Wicklow, Ireland.

Saunders Grove would have made an impression on John James. The house had been built in 1716 by Morley Saunders MP and in a manner traditional for the time, the large garden, complete with grand steps and cascades, faced along a formal canal. Unfortunately, there is little left of the place the Crow family would have known so well, as the original house was burnt down in 1923 and replaced with a smaller building. During their time at Saunders Grove the family occupied several rooms in the main house but they most likely also inhabited Grove Cottage, a modest house situated some 200 yards from the main building.

John James was the eldest son of Caroline and John, although, apart from Frederick, he would also have many other siblings, all of whom were born while the family lived in Baltinglass. Their names and birthdates are listed below:

Robert Henry (Known as Harry) born 14th May 1885
William George (Known as George) born 21st November 1887
Minnie born 19th January 1890

William (Known as Bill) born 12th may 1892
Albert Edgar born 13th April 1894
Annie and Florence (twins) born 16th December 1895
Charles born 11th December 1899

John James and Frederick's brothers and sisters were all christened by the Rector Reverend John Usher of St Mary's church in Baltinglass, where the family worshipped.

The Crow family fitted in well at Saunders Grove and were quickly welcomed into the Irish community. Mrs Dolly Crowe, the daughter-in-law of William George, recently relayed an incident that reflects this to Doreen and Robin Pannett. With such a large family, times were sometimes tough and as a result they kept a number of hens in order to supplement the family's food supplies. One night, all the hens were stolen and upon hearing of the theft the Rector announced in his Sunday service that the perpetrator would be eternally damned should he not return the hens at once. No more than two nights later all the hens were returned, including one, which had already been plucked and prepared for the oven!

Two further things of note happened during the family's time at Saunders Grove. The first was that at some point John decided to add an 'e' to the family surname. The second was that John taught his eldest son, John James, to use a rifle. Together they spent time shooting rabbits and catching fish, skills that would serve the young man well in his later life.

Chapter Two

Before the War 1897 – 1914

BEFORE THE turn of the century, regiments in the British Army were still named after their Colonels. For instance, Colonel Farrington of the Coldstream Guards first raised Farrington's Foot in 1694. The same was true in 1701, when Viscount Charlemont raised the Charlemont's Foot. In 1751, Regiments first became numbered and so Farrington's Foot became known as the 29th and Charlemont's Foot the 36th. In 1781, County titles were introduced and Farrington's Foot duly became known as the 29th Worcestershire Regiment, and Charlemont's Foot the 36th Herefordshire Regiment. By 1881, the two had been amalgamated and became known as the 1st and 2nd Battalions of the Worcestershire Regiment.

It was to this Regiment, on 1st July 1897, the year of Queen Victoria's Diamond Jubilee, that John James enlisted, quite literally following in his father's footsteps. Prior to this, John James had worked as a footman in Dublin. Deciding that was not the life for him, he initially signed on for a short service engagement and was promptly posted to Norton

Barracks near Worcester. John James' enrolment card lists his Regimental Number as 4959 and describes him as being 5 ft 6ins tall, weighing 123lbs, with a fresh complexion, grey eyes and brown hair; much like his father before him. John James' potential first became apparent only thirty-five days after joining up when he was promoted to Lance Corporal and although when he was posted to the 1st Battalion he had to temporarily relinquish his rank, it was soon awarded again on 8th September 1898.

During 1900, Britain was involved in the South African War and this conflict saw an expansion of the British Army. In February of that year two additional regular Battalions, namely the 3rd and 4th, were created at Aldershot and added to the Worcestershire Regiment. The Battalions were soon quartered together at Blenheim Barracks, North Camp. By now, the

John Crowe and his wife, Margaret Ellen.

Regiment consisted of the 1st, 2nd, 3rd and 4th Regular Battalions along with the 5th and 6th Militia Battalions and two volunteer Battalions, which later became known as the 7th and 8th Territorial Battalions. On 23rd February 1900, John James was posted to the 4th Battalion and promoted again, this time to Corporal. After being posted to Aldershot, John James' career continued to blossom with further promotions in 1901 to Lance Sergeant and then four months later to Sergeant.

Prior to enlisting in the army John James had met Margaret Ellen Langron while working in Dublin. They had stayed in touch and in early 1902, knowing that he would soon be sent overseas, John James returned to Ireland to marry his sweetheart. Margaret Ellen and John James were married in the Catholic Chapel of St James in Dublin on 3rd February 1902. At the time, Margaret was living in a small house at 20 Woodfield Terrace, Inchore Road, Dublin and although she had lived elsewhere in the intervening years, this was the same house in which she had been born on 20th August 1874. Margaret was one of seven children born to her parents Hugh, an engine fitter, and Anne (nee Tyrrell). The eldest was Mary Josephine, born 18th August 1872, followed by Margaret and then Annie. The twins, Christine and Joseph Christopher, in turn followed them and the youngest of the girls, Ellen Nellie, born on 10th July 1890, eventually married John James' brother, Robert Henry. Hugh and Anne's youngest child was John who, like so many other young men of his generation, would fall on the battlefields of the First World War.

Just two weeks after John James and Margaret were married, the 4th Battalion set sail aboard HMS Harlech Castle, arriving in Bermuda on 4th March 1902. It is not known whether Margaret travelled with John James or made her way separately a few months later, but they would enjoy their stay in the Caribbean. Whilst there, the 4th Battalion was employed guarding Boer prisoners from the South African War and they also received their Regimental Colours from the Bermudan Governor, Sir Henry Geary. The training that John James had received from his father at Saunders Grove proved profitable when the 4th Battalion won the Challenge cup at a joint Naval and Military Rifle Meeting. Again, John displayed the skills that were to serve him well only a few years later.

Challenge Cup. 3rd Battalion Worcestershire Regiment. Top row (left to right) Sgt Crowe, Color Sgt Stone, Sgt Nash. Bottom row (left to right) Color Sgt Stanley, Color Sgt Parker, Lance Corporal Band.

In 1903, after a happy two years spent in Bermuda, the Battalion moved to the West Indies. Detachments went to Jamaica and St Lucia, John James and Margaret sailed to Barbados on the Dunera. Barbados proved to be a memorable place for the Crowes, as their first child, Annie Margaret, was born there on 30th April 1904.

Later that year, John James was promoted again to Colour Sergeant. He also continued to prove his shooting prowess, winning the Inter-Colonial Rifle Cup for two years in a row. It appears that, despite the difficulty of living in the tropics, the young family enjoyed their stay in Barbados. Margaret had

The Henry Whitehead Cup team. John Crowe, front, left.

the help of a nanny and she was often seen around the island on her bicycle. However, on 4th January 1906, John James was posted back to the Depot at Norton Barracks in England.

It was here, a month later, that he was promoted again to Colour Sergeant, Instructor of Musketry, a position he would hold for nearly two years, during which time he and Margaret had two further children. Mary Josephine, named after her aunt, was born at Norton near Worcester on 14th May 1906 and baptised the same month at the Church of St George. On 10th October 1907, John James was born,

Colour Sergeant J.J Crowe with Margaret and their first child, Anne.

named after his father although always referred to as Jack. Jack was born in Dublin and christened at the same chapel in which John James and Margaret had been married. Strangely, Jack does not have a birth certificate and his birth was never officially registered. It is not known why; perhaps it was due to John James' regiment being hastily posted to South Africa.

Captain J. J Crowe V.C.

At the time, the native tribes in South Africa had become a nuisance to the British and it was decided that the British military presence there should be increased. At the same time, the British Army was going through some major changes as it adapted to warfare in the twentieth century. Indiscriminate volley fire was being phased out in favour of more accurate marksmanship and John James' shooting prowess meant that he was in high demand. On 1st November 1907, he had resigned his position as Instructor of Musketry and been posted to 3rd Battalion, based at Mandora Barracks near Aldershot. Over the years, the 3rd Battalion had gained respect for their musketry proficiency, winning the Whitehead Cup in 1903 and the Queen Victoria Cup in 1903, 1904 and 1905.

This string of successes meant that the 3rd Battalion was regarded as the best shooting Battalion in Great Britain, making them an ideal candidate for duty overseas and on 27th November 1907, the Battalion and their families duly set sail for Africa. The arduous nature of this journey cannot be underestimated. At the time, Jack was only six weeks old, Mary was barely eighteen months and Annie was less than four years old. Keeping all three children safe, happy and occupied on a busy troop ship for days on end, as it travelled through the Bay of Biscay, was no mean feat for the women that accompanied their husbands. The dangers aboard such a ship are highlighted by the

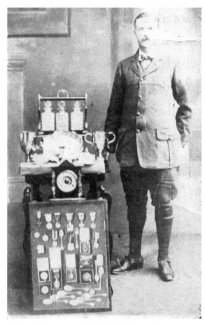

John Crowe with his shooting medals and trophies.

way that Annie was tethered to one of the ship's masts as she played on deck, keeping her safe from harm.

Queen Victoria Cup 1913. J. J Crowe is seated first left.

Three weeks after leaving Southampton the ship docked at Capetown. During their stay in Cape Colony, the 3rd Battalion were stationed at Wynberg, south of Capetown and the magnificent Table Mountain. The young families spent Christmas that year at Grooke Schaur, worrying about the threat posed by the native tribes, a threat that thankfully never materialised. A year later, the Battalion was back in England, arriving at Dover at the beginning of October 1908.

Christmas Day 1907 in South Africa, Grooke Schaur.

The British experience in Africa had convinced any remaining doubters of the need for change. The army was still one that had more in common with that which took to the field at Waterloo than of a modern, twentieth century fighting force. As a result, many changes were instigated, greatly aided by the appointment of Lord Kitchener to Commander-in-Chief. Under his direction the training of all units was standardised and the severe, but necessary. 'Kitchener Test' was implemented. This examination required units to undertake a long forced march in full kit, followed by a practice attack, a test that quickly ensured the proficiency of all fighting units in the British Army.

The reliance on fast and accurate rifle skills remained high on the agenda. The 3rd Battalion achieved this in 1909, they again won the Whitehead Cup. Colour Sergeant John James Crowe was on the team. Individually, John James achieved success, too, winning the Shooting Cup at Dover for three years in succession. He also participated in the Queens Cup, a competition organised by the Society of Miniature Rifle Clubs. Along with his undoubted marksmanship, John James was also an athlete of some note, competing in several cross-country events, as well as in obstacle races and track events. This led him to win the Athletic Cup in 1912 and be crowned the finest athlete in his Battalion that year. He also enjoyed other sports such as hockey, although he refrained from the more social side of sports, as he remained a 'teetotal' throughout his life and a member of the Army Temperance Society.

Throughout the years, John and Caroline Crowe had stayed at Saunders Grove, not leaving there until around 1905. On their return to England they purchased a small terraced house at number 28 Dorset Street, Reading and lived there with a number of their children until the end of the First World War. Life, however, was not easy for the Crowes and money was always scarce. John James recalled visiting them once on leave and when he enquired as to why his brother, William, was running about in his bare feet he was informed that that his brother did not even own a pair of shoes!

John James advised his brother to join the army, who would at least give him a pair of decent boots, and in due course, William took his brother's advice, joining the Worcester Regiment in July 1911. Years later, William used to tell his sons about the hard time his brother gave him whenever they met up during their army days, although as William was attached to the 2nd Battalion this rarely happened.

Whilst performing his army duties, John James also found time to pursue his academic studies and in March 1911 he was awarded an Army First Class Certificate of Education. He attained a proficient standard in arithmetic and composition and was also more than competent in geography, map reading and modern English history.

In 1912, the 3rd Battalion was moved to Tidworth, where they took their place in the 7th Brigade as part of the 3rd Division. The following year was to be another significant period for John James and Margaret. The 3rd Battalion won the Queen Victoria Cup for the fourth time, as well as the Roberts Cup, which was presented by Field Marshal Earl Roberts of Kandahar himself, the last time that the great man would personally award the trophy to the winning team. John James played an integral role in both these victories, further cementing his reputation as a crack marksman. The awards kept on coming for John James and 3rd Battalion, as they won several trophies at the Salisbury District Rifle Meeting, including the Inter-Regimental Cup and the Sergeant's Cup. On 1st October, John James was promoted to Company Sergeant Major and on the final day of 1913, Christine Ellen, the youngest daughter of Margaret and John James, was born. The following year would bring a World War, which would change the Crowe's lives forever.

Chapter Three

The First World War

August 1914 – September 1917

DESPITE BELGIUM'S neutrality, German forces crossed the border on 3rd August 1914. The response from Great Britain was unanimous and she declared war on Germany at 11 am the following day. That evening, 2nd and 3rd Battalions, Worcestershire Regiment received their mobilisation orders. The following weeks saw all ranks preparing for war. Each Battalion was brought up to fighting strength as it received the necessary reservists, weapons, equipment and ammunition. Officers and men were all required to undergo medical examinations to assess their suitability for active deployment, horses were requisitioned and regimental property, including the Colours of both Battalions were placed in safe keeping. The Colours were transported to Worcester, under the watchful eye of special escorts, and placed in the care of the Dean and Chapter to be preserved in the city's cathedral until such time as the Battalions needed them again.

Mobilization was completed during the second week of August and during this time the two Battalions stood fast awaiting further orders. Despite the meticulous preparations, getting an army ready for war proved to be a difficult business. Every man was required to be issued with two pairs of boots, but due to the creation of the 'New Armies' equipment was often in short supply, which in turn meant that the second pair of boots (something that would prove to be invaluable in Europe) had been withdrawn from most units. Consequently, both the 2nd and 3rd Battalions left for France with just one pair apiece. It was a shortage that both brothers would find a severe trial.

Early in the morning of 13th August, the 2nd Battalion left Aldershot for Southampton Docks. There they boarded ships and steamed across the channel that night, reaching Boulogne on the afternoon of 14th. The 3rd Battalion followed close behind but owing to the state of the tide the SS Bosnian had to anchor off Le Havre until the morning of the 16th before she was allowed to proceed up the River Seine to Rouen. For many of the men, the trip up the Seine was an exciting one. As they sailed along the river past the rolling forests and picturesque Norman villages, cheered all the way by the crowds that thronged the river's banks, they could have little idea of the inferno in which they would soon find themselves.

At 9pm, the Battalion finally reached Rouen and they passed their first night in France in a long shed sited by the dock. The next day, they marched through the streets of Rouen to the Gard du Nord and boarded trains for the Front. It was to be a baptism of fire and both the 2nd and 3rd Battalions saw action at the Battle of Mons on 24th August 1914. Both suffered their first casualties that day. They would not be their last.

On arrival in France the strength of 3rd Battalion was 32 officers, 987 other ranks and 61 horses, but John James was not among their number. On August 5th, one day after war was declared, he had been promoted to Quarter-Master Sergeant, a new rank for the British Army, the next day he embarked for France. For the next three years he would be stationed at Number 29 Infantry Base. BEF Depot, near Rouen.

John James' medals included the 1914 Star with Bar. The medal had been awarded to all men of the British and Indian Expeditionary Force who had actually served in France or Belgium on the establishment of a unit between 5th August and midnight on 22nd/23rd November 1914. On 19th October 1919, it was announced that the King had approved the issue of a bar to those already awarded the 1914 Star 'who had actually served under fire of the enemy in France or Belgium'. John James' bar therefore implies that he went up to the front on at least one occasion, probably more, before 22nd November 1914.

Although Margaret had accompanied her husband overseas on previous occasions, the outbreak of war meant that this was no longer possible. Shortly before the war had begun Margaret had left the married quarter at Tidworth with her four children and moved to Brighton in Sussex. They initially moved to 120 Upper Lewes Road, the home of George Crowe and his wife, Louise. A few years later, Margaret and the children moved to Dudley House in Dudley Road, Brighton, where Margaret would live for the rest of her life.

By the summer of 1914, Annie was aged ten, Mary was eight, Jack was nearly seven and Christine was just eight months old. It is not known why Margaret decided to move to Brighton, as she had no known connections with the town, although it can be assumed that living near to her brother-in-law was the main draw. Even so, setting up home in a strange town, without the help of her husband, would have been a formidable task.

Margaret was a Roman Catholic and her faith undoubtedly helped her. She insisted that the children attended church once each Saturday and three times on Sunday they worshipped at St Joseph's Church at the bottom of Elm Grove. Despite Jack's less than enthusiastic attitude towards the church, he dutifully obeyed his mother's wishes and was an altar boy for seven years before joining the choir. At Christmas he would enthral the congregation with his solo performances of 'Adeste Fidelis' and his elder sister, Annie, was also an accomplished singer, serving as part of the choir and performing her own solo of 'Ave Maria'. Annie was evidently a talented musician and singer and she was awarded several certificates at the School of Music both for her singing and piano recitals.

While at Dudley House, Jack found another task that irked him to the same degree as the choir. At 7 o'clock each morning he was required to take the family goat to graze in a field about half a mile from their home. Poor jack also had to retrieve the animal each evening, something that he particularly disliked on the cold winter nights. On their return home the young boy also had to milk the animal and when he wasn't at school he was kept busy working in the family garden.

Meanwhile, back in France, the war continued apace. On 15th January 1915, John James was promoted again to Warrant Officer Class II and while he was based at Rouen he sent them regular postcards home. Several that he sent to Mary still exist and the message he wrote on one, post-marked 29th November 1916, reads as follows:

Dear Mary,
How are you? I hope you have not got chilblains yet. Keep your
hands very dry by rubbing them well with one hand rubbing the

other after washing them. I hope you are doing plenty of work. Mother will tell me.

Best love from Dad.

A Postcard that Warrant Officer Crowe sent to his daughter, Mary, on the 29th November 1916, telling her to keep her hands dry to avoid chilblains.

John James was by no means the only member of his family to serve in the war. Three of his brothers; George, William and Albert, as well as his two brother-in-laws, Joseph and John, had also joined the army. George was a member of the 12th Divisional Cycling Corps and served in France. William was with the 4th Battalion, Worcester regiment and by 1915 was an Army Scout (First Class) and the best shot in his company. The 4th Battalion had returned to England from Burma on 1st February 1915 and after disembarking at Avonmouth they spent a month at Banbury before marching to Leamington, where they were assigned to 88th Brigade, which was part of the 29th Division. On 12th March, the Division was inspected by King George V near Dunchurch and by the 22nd they were back at Avonmouth, embarking for service overseas.

Although their official destination was kept secret, their orders issued at Avonmouth were to proceed to Gibraltar, it was widely regarded that they were headed for the Dardanelles. And so it was that on 27th March, the convoy entered the Mediterranean and steamed on for Malta, where they stopped briefly to take on coal and stores. On Easter Sunday, 4th April, the convoy reached Alexandria but the harbour was so crowded that the transports laden down with the 4th Battalion had to wait for three days before they could berth. The companies finally disembarked on 6th April and marched through the streets of Alexandria to a camp on the shore at Mustapha Pasha. By Nightfall on the 8th, they were again onboard ship, this time the large transport vessel, Aragon.

On the night of the 11th April they set sail and after passing by the Aegean Islands they reached their destination on 13th; the Bay of Mudos, off the island of Lemnos. The Dardanelles had indeed been their destination and on 21st April orders were received stipulating that the 29th Division, along with several other divisions, make a landing on the end of the Gallipoli Peninsular, near to Cape Helles. Most of the 4th Battalion landed on the first day of the assault, 25th April, a day that later would become known as ANZAC Day. It was intended that they should land on 'V Beach', but it was quickly realised that the place was a veritable death trap and as a result they were diverted to 'W Beach', where the Lancaster Fusiliers had effected a bridgehead.

Fighting on the Gallipoli Peninsula was a bloody affair and one that continued throughout 1915. Units involved in combat suffered heavy casualties and the same was true for the 4th Battalion. By August 1915, the Battalion was so depleted in numbers that it was amalgamated with the remaining elements of the Hampshires and the Royal Scotts, in order to form a complete Battalion. Amongst the many casualties was William Crowe, although luckily he was only wounded and was sent back to Egypt to recuperate. He spent Christmas that year with the composite Battalion at Damarhur in Egypt and in January 1916, the Gallipoli campaign was called off and the remaining troops were evacuated in an operation, the success of which belied the abject failure of the entire campaign.

In March 1916, the 29th Division received orders to proceed to France and on 15th March they boarded the transport ship 'Transylvania' bound for Marseilles. From the French port they were trained to Port Remy, where they arrived in the early hours of March 23rd. Meanwhile, the 4th Battalion entered the trenches at Mary Redan, south of Beaumont Hamel, in the heart of the Somme battlefield. In August, William Crowe was given leave and on 26th August he married Daisy Chigney in Reading, a girl he had known for many years, before promptly returning to the 4th Battalion in France.

John James' extended family also served throughout the war. John Langron, John James' brother-in-law, served as a Private with the Royal Dublin Fusiliers and he too saw action on 25th April at Gallipoli when 1st Battalion lead the assault on V Beach. It was a strongly defended position and the assault party met stiff resistance, resulting in heavy casualties, among them was John Langron. John was killed that day and is buried in V Beach Cemetery, located at the bottom of the grassy slope that meets the cliff edge between Sedd el Bahr and Cape Helles. Like many other men who died in the war, he does not have an identified grave, but is commemorated on Special Memorial B, Number 18.

Albert Edgar Crowe served as a Private soldier with 2nd Battalion Grenadier Guards. His last engagement with the enemy was during the Battle of the Somme. The infamous battle raged from 1st July to 18th November 1916 and Albert was killed in action on 16th September. The battle was one of the most costly of the war for the British, with an estimated number of combat deaths totalling some 125,000 men. Like John Langron, Albert also has no known grave, a testament to the destructive power of the modern weaponry deployed in the conflict. He is commemorated along with more than 72,000 others on the Memorial to the Missing at Thiepval. His name can be found on Pier 8, Face D.

John Langron's brother, and John James' brother-in-law, Joseph Christopher Langron also served in France during the war. Thankfully, he survived, despite being gassed, and after the war moved to Canada, where he lived until he died, aged ninety-seven.

In April 1917, John James was awarded the Long Service Medal, as well as the Good Conduct Medal, the requirements for which were to have completed eighteen years service and have an unblemished character record. Testament indeed to the type of man John James undoubtedly was. The war quickly became a massive drain on resources and produce such as fresh vegetables were always in short supply. To combat these shortages, John James, while stationed at Rouen, developed a 4-acre vegetable garden at the depot. As a reward for this initiative, in October 1917, the French government awarded him the Diplome d'Honneur et d'Encouragement.

At the beginning of September 1917, John James left No 29 Infantry Base at Rouen and on his departure the Commanding Officer wrote the following testimonial for him:

No 29 Infantry Base,
B.E.F Depot,
France.
25th August 1917.

Q.M. Segt Crowe, 3 Worcester Regt. has been my Q.M. Segt. since the beginning of the war. At the commencement no Q.M. was appointed, he did all the Q.M's work as well as his own. He is hard working, reliable, trustworthy and very willing. He has in every direction worked to my entire satisfaction. I have now a flower garden & vegetable garden extending over about 4-acres. These have been under Q.M.S. Crowe's charge, in fact he has done most of the work. The flower garden is a picture and is considered to be the best in Rouen. The vegetable garden is also the best in all the camps. This is entirely due to Crowe's work. He is leaving me to take up Segt Majorship of his Battalion. I need hardly say I shall miss him.
Signed
Lt Colonel
Commander No 29 I. B. Depot.

September 1917 – March 1918

On 6th September 1917, John James was promoted to Regimental Sergeant-Major and he promptly rejoined 3rd Battalion Worcester Regiment. At the time, they were in the 7th Brigade, which was part of the 25th Division, spending time in the Divisional Reserve at Dickebusch. However, soon orders arrived for the 25th Division to be transferred from the Second to the First Army, requiring them to move back behind the lines for a period of training at Burbure.

On 4th October, with their training completed, 3rd Battalion marched forward again and after dark relieved the 17th Middlesex in the trenches just to the east of Le Plantin. Demonstrating the multi-national aspect of the First World War, the left flank of the Battalion found itself next to the Portuguese in one of the quieter sectors of the line. Worryingly, the Battalion was spread thinly, as their position stretched across some 2,000 yards of the front. More worrying still, the weather was expected to be dreadful that winter, which would cause a great deal of suffering for the men, but thankfully, that October the weather remained relatively quiet and so to did the line. From 5th November until 10th November, the 3rd Battalion and the 10th Loyal North Lancashire alternatively held the line, alternating between the front, and the support positions at Windy Corner, or the Reserve stationed at Gorre.

10th November that year was a notable day in the history of Worcester Regiment, as 3rd Battalion was transferred from 7th Brigade in which it had served continuously for over six years, through both war and peace. The 2nd Royal Irish Rifles had been transferred from the 25th Division to the 36th (Ulster) Division and being left with only three Regular Battalions in his Division, General Banbridge had decided to distribute them one to each Brigade. Accordingly, 3rd Division was transferred to the 74th Brigade in place of the Irishmen. After bidding farewell to their old comrades, 3rd Battalion set out from Windy Corner towards Annequin, on 10th November 1917. There they came into the support position for their new Brigade, which was currently holding the line just south of the La Bassee Canal. By the 16th, 3rd Battalion had moved forward to the trenches facing Auchy, located astride the railway line, in order to relieve the 11th Lancashire Fusiliers, the right-hand most Battalion of the 74th Brigade. On 23rd, they moved back again to the support positions at Annequin and three days later they went into Reserve at Beuvry.

Before dawn on the 30th November, the Battalion was again sent forward up the line and this time they would be in for a hard time of it. At 2.30am, the enemy guns burst into life, raining shells down on the Battalion's positions. After an hour and a half, a German raiding party rushed the positions of the left-hand company. This resulted in a bitter bombing fight in which Captain A Vint and 2nd Lieut W.N Bretell, along with a small band of men, attacked the enemy with grenades and managed to drive them from the Battalion's positions. During the encounter one enemy soldier was killed and 2nd Lieut Bretell was severely wounded. Not long after, a second attempt was made, this was easily repulsed by rifle and machine gun fire before the enemy reached the British trenches. Despite the German's failure, the artillery bombardment had caused severe damage to the British positions and this was further compounded by a third attempt the following day. Trench raids were a common occurrence on the Western Front and they were universally hated and often ended in disaster.

After sleepless nights enduring the German attacks, the Battalion was faced with the prospect of repairing the trenches under harassing fire from the enemy, a dangerous and arduous task. Thankfully, the next evening, 2nd December, the Battalion handed over their positions to the 1/5th Leicestershire and proceeded to march to Chocques, where they boarded trains heading south.

On 5th December, 3rd Battalion arrived at Achiet-le-Grand and headed for the camp near Achiet-le-Petit. The respite was brief and on 7th December the 74th Brigade moved forward again, relieving the 9th Brigade in the line facing Queant and Pronville. 3rd Battalion initially remained in support near Lagincourt and after a further three days in Reserve, they moved up the line to take charge of the nearby trenches. The 3rd's new position faced a section of the formidable Hindenburg Line, a massive defensive system, which here embraced the ruined village of Queant. The danger of the Hindenburg Line defences was such that No Man's Land stretched for almost a mile, offering some respite from the impressive fortifications. On 19th December, after six days in the line, which were gratefully uneventful, 3rd Battalion was relieved and moved back down the line to Beugnatre. Again, the respite was brief and on 23rd December the Battalion returned to the same positions, spending the bitterly cold Christmas of 1917 shivering in the snow, watching the Hindenburg Line through the gloom, knowing that sooner or later it would have to be overcome.

The following nights were cold and illuminated by a full moon and a white frost that covered No Man's Land. It made attacks and trench raids particularly dangerous, something that was epitomised on 27th when a patrol set out just before dawn. Silhouetted against the frosty ground they were quickly spotted and a German machine gun promptly opened fire. Two were killed and three more wounded, with the survivors forced to crawl back to their trenches to report the debacle. Leaving dead comrades out in the wilds of No Man's Land was not only bad for morale, they may also have had information valuable to the enemy about their person. As a result, a party of six men, lead by 2nd Lieut Shaw, crawled out of the British trenches after dark to retrieve the bodies of their fallen friends. The operation was hazardous in the extreme as the party of six had to crawl over the snow under the light of a full moon. With great difficulty, Lieut Shaw managed to retrieve the bodies of the dead and bring the wounded back to the relative safety of the British trenches.

That evening, the Battalion was relieved and they spent the next three days in the support lines, before returning to the front lines on New Year's Eve. After four days, the Battalion moved back to the Brigade Reserve at Beugnatre, where they enjoyed a slightly delayed, but thoroughly deserved, Christmas dinner of pork, plum pudding and plenty of beer.

Three days later, normality resumed and the Battalion found itself stationed in the line in front of Pronville. For the next five weeks they rotated in and out of the position, alternating between the trenches and the support and reserve positions. The weather that January was appalling and between the 15th and 16th of the month it rained almost continually. Consequently, the sides of the trenches began to collapse and by the 17th the trenches had become completely impassable, requiring all movement to take place in the open. As a result, the British provided easier targets for the enemy's artillery, which were particularly active during the period, further adding to the misery. During the miserable period between 9th January to 8th February little of importance happened on the line, nevertheless 3rd Battalion still suffered 7 casualties, a reflection on the attritional nature of trench warfare.

At the end of January 1918, a general reorganisation of all Infantry Brigades took place, which, amongst other things, entailed an alteration to the method used for holding the line. The new approach required a focus on 'defence in depth', something the Germans had carried out with a great deal of success for most of the war. As a result, when 3rd Battalion retook its place in the line again, on 26th January, the four companies of the Battalion had to extend across a length of line measuring some 1,500 yards. This required that the men were spread very thin; causing a great strain on the nerves, as a constant vigilance was employed to stop an attack that many assumed was inevitable.

However, on 11th February, the 25th Division was again relieved, this time by 6th Division, and they proceeded to move back down the line into reserve positions near Achiet-le-Grand. 3rd Battalion remained there for the next month during which they carried out training exercises and recuperated. It was a sorely needed rest, but during their time at Achiet-le-Grand, Lieutenant Colonel A. Whitty, one of the best-loved figures in the Battalion, left the unit, to great consternation.

It was during this period of training that George Crowe, of the 12th Divisional Cycling Corps happened to be passing his brother's location. Hearing the unmistakable voice of his brother issuing orders, he pulled over and the two brothers spent a brief time together before each resumed his duties. It was to be the only time during the war that the brothers would meet.

As February turned to March, so too did the tide of the war. Germany was suffering, both on the battlefield and at home, where the Royal Navy's blockade of her ports was slowly starving the country of raw materials and food. America had entered the war and it was only a matter of time until their almost unlimited resources would take to the field. Together, this meant that a final, desperate German push was becoming more and more likely. To meet the perceived threat many troops waiting in support were moved closer to the front and among them was 3rd Battalion Worcestershire Regiment. It had been intended that the 25th Division, upon completing a period training in reserve, should again take its place on the front line at Pronville. However, due to the imminent threat, and the new approach to defence in depth, the 25th were ordered to remain in reserve and be prepared to engage in a counter-attack if required. On 13th March, 74th Brigade were moved to the forward area near Fremicourt and 3rd Worcestershire was sent to camp between Favreuil and Beugnatre.

On 18th March, John James Crowe was granted a permanent commission in the Worcester Regiment and so resigned from the Colours after 20 years and 261 days of service. John James had served with distinction and as a result of his bravery during the period from 25th September 1917 to 24th February 1918 he was mentioned in Sir Douglas Haig's despatch from France, dated 7th April 1918 (London Gazette dated 23rd July 1918).

April 1918

On 1st April 1918, the newly promoted 2nd Lieut John James Crowe was posted to the 2nd Battalion Worcestershire Regiment. Within days of his deployment he was given a field rank of acting Captain and acting Adjutant. The 2nd Battalion was in 100th Brigade, which was part of the 33rd Division. At the beginning of April 1918, the Battalion found itself stationed in the Ypres Salient, but orders were soon received for the 33rd Division to be relieved from the line and sent back for a brief period of training before being sent to reinforce the Third Army. Accordingly, on 5th April, the Battalion departed from Ypres and for the next two days marched to Peselhoch, where they boarded trains for Tincques. From there the Battalion marched to their billets at Izel-les-Hameau, near Penin, where they settled down to complete a period of training and enjoy a brief respite from the line.

With their training complete, the 100th Brigade began its march south toward the Somme on the morning of 10th April. The 2nd Worcestershire led the way to the rendezvous with Third Army, but as they reached Manin a sudden halt was called. They had received orders to return to the billets they had just left, so the remainder of the day was spent retracing their steps to Izel.

The rumours of the big German offensive were rife and the air was thick with tension. Shortly after dark orders came instructing the fighting troops of the Brigade to make their way to Aubigny station with all possible speed. The trains left at midnight and after a long and uncomfortable journey the 2nd Worcestershires arrived at Caestre, near Bailleul early on the morning of Thursday 11th April. The scene must have been one of chaos as the Allied armies prepared to stem the German advance. On arrival at the station the men were greeted by the sight of a vast line of lorries and buses waiting to transport the companies of the 2nd Battalion forward to Meteren. During their journey they encountered the realities of what was happening on the front lines. A steady stream of haggard looking refugees passed them by, heading in the other direction, away from the ceaseless barrages that had driven them from their homes.

On arrival at Meteren, the Battalion joined up with the rest of the 100th Brigade, where they were informed that the brigade had been placed under the temporary command of the 25th Division. Around noon, the 2nd Worcestershires and the 16th K.R.R.C were ordered to advance and they marched off towards the sound of the guns. As they approached the steady stream of refugees grew thinner and thinner, replaced by bursting shells and the staccato sound of machine gun fire. When they finally reached Bailleul, they found a shattered town under almost continuous bombardment. The men were forced to thread their way through the shattered ruins, trying as best they could to avoid the collapsing buildings by keeping to the middle of the streets. Once through the other side they marched east of Baileul, into open country and towards the imposing Ravelsberg ridge. Here, at around 4 o'clock in the afternoon, the men halted their march, discarded their packs, extra ammunition was issued and each man confronted his thoughts as he prepared for battle.

The Commanding Officer of IX Corps was so impressed by the actions of 2nd Battalion during the defence of Neuve Eglise that he determined it warranted the issue of a special order, which is reproduced below:

IX Corps Special Order No 3
The following record is to be made of the action described below.

2nd Battalion Worcestershire Regiment
Neuve Eglise 11-14 April 1918

On the evening of the 11th April, the 2nd Battalion the Worcestershire Regiment took over a section of the line to the east of Neuve Eglise. The night was spent in strengthening and concealing the defences of the position. The following morning, two strong patrols were pushed out and quickly came into touch with superior enemy forces, which they fought to a standstill, inflicting heavy losses. They were withdrawn later, but not until the enemy had been obliged to considerably strengthen his patrols and to postpone his impending attack.

During the day, enemy activity greatly increased and the Battalion patrols were constantly engaged in stopping small parties who were endeavouring to work their way into the lines. At 7.30 in the evening, after heavy artillery and machine gun preparation, the enemy developed an attack to both the right and left of the line held, breaking through the right. He was ejected and the position restored. Early on the morning of the 13th he again attacked to the right, reached NEUVE EGLISE village and thus took the Battalion line in the rear. An immediate counter attack not only turned the enemy out of the village, but led to the annihilation of the forces which had gained a footing there and to the destruction of its machine guns.

At 6pm, the enemy attacked in great strength on the left, and the whole Battalion withdrew fighting to a new position. The Mairie was organised as a strong point; the garrison effectively dealt with enemy parties, which had crept up to the main crossroads on the right.

During the night, attack after attack was launched against the Battalion, and eventually touch was lost with the companies holding the left. They were last heard of holding on against overwhelming odds, fighting it out to the last.

Meanwhile, the enemy had crept nearer and nearer to the Mairie, which was held by Battalion Head-quarters. At dawn on the 14th, he was seen to be occupying NEUVE EGLISE in strength, and soon after the Mairie was completely surrounded. 2nd Lieut JOHNSON at once volunteered to try and work his way through to the Brigade and report the situation. His gallant attempt was unsuccessful and he did not return.

Clever manoeuvring and well directed fire forced the enemy to relinquish his hold and retire to the high ground to the right and to the church on the left. 2nd Lieut CROWE with a small party worked round the flank of the former position and surprising the enemy, forced him further up the rise. The success of this feint was completed by a very daring sortie led by the same officer and 2nd Lieut POINTON, and supported by accurate fire from the Mairie, which compelled the Germans to withdraw to the centre of the village.

Early in the afternoon the enemy was observed to be preparing for a violent attack upon the Mairie. A withdrawal was decided upon, and in spite of heavy fire was carried out without loss to the railway, where British troops had already taken up their positions.

By the well-planned and spirited defence under very difficult conditions, the Battalion kept the enemy at bay for three days, without rest, and in the face of greatly superior numbers. Fine patrol work delayed and harassed the preparation of attacks, rapidity of counter-attacks, coupled with skilful disposition of forces in response to every enemy move, obliged him time after time to relinquish his gains; tenacity when all seemed hopeless opened a way to safety; while daring and gallantry of individual officers and men did much to prevent the effective use of larger forces at the enemy's disposal and extracted a heavy price for every yard gained.

(Signed) B.L MONTGOMERY
for Brig Gen
General Staff, IX Corps

The following awards were given to Officers and men of the 2nd Battalion for their actions during the defence of Neuve Eglise:

Acting Lieut Colonel G. J. L Stoney	Commanding Officer	D.S.O.
Acting Captain J. J Crowe	Acting Adjutant	V.C.
Lieut C. S Jagger		M.C.

Lieut F. S Orford	Signals Officer	M.C
2nd Lieut A. Johnson		bar to M.C
2nd Lieut H. J Nicklin		M.C
2nd Lieut A. C POINTON		M.C
2nd Lieut J. Turley		M.C
2nd Lieut V. L Vernon		M.C
C.Q.M.S A. Trotman		D.C.M
Sergeant R. V. Clare		D.C.M
Sergeant E. Edwards		D.C.M
Sergeant F. W Day		D.C.M
Corporal S. Wilkinson		D.C.M
Private R.F Bough		D.C.M

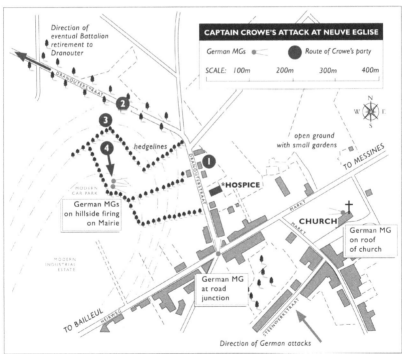

*NOTE - The HOSPICE was the building that earlier writers had mistakenly referred to as 'The Mairie'

Captain Crowe embarked on a sortie to try and clear a route for the Worcesters to withdraw to the British lines.

He led seven men to clear the enemy out of a cow shed just north of the Mairie (1). After that they attempted to fire at the enemy position on the rise in the meadow to the west, but their position in the road was enfiladed by enemy fire from the south. Captain Crowe, taking two men with him, crawled to his right (north) along the road gutter until they were unobserved by the enemy position due north of it (2). From here they crept up a hedge line onto the rise itself.

All three of them opened rapid fire and dispersed the enemy lining the hedge (3). Those hours on the firing points in Dover and at Bisley had certainly paid off. Two machine guns manned by seven or eight of the enemy were still firing but Crowe and his two comrades rushed them, shooting as they ran (4).

One of his men was killed but Crowe reached the guns and the enemy fled. With their rear now secured, the Worcesters, carrying their wounded, were able to withdraw without further loss. Their desperate defense of Neuve Eglise had delayed the enemy advance for a vital three days between the 11th and 14th April. The Germans were finally stopped a mile from the gates of Ypres.

After the war, a series of articles were published in the magazine of the Worcestershire Regiment, 'The Green 'Un' describing the exploits of the officers and men of the Regiment who were awarded the Victoria Cross during the First World War. However, John James only fully recounted his experiences to Reverend Tanner in a letter he wrote a few months before he died, in 1964. The Reverend had previously written to John James to enquire about his exploits that day in April 1918 and John James' reply is printed:

A copy of Gilbert Haliday's painting showing 2nd Lieut J. J Crowe in action.

November 11th 1964

Dear Padre,

Many thanks for your long and very nice letter. Now you want to know what happened at Neuve Eglise. True a long time ago, but I have fought that battle over more than once but I don't think we could have done better. On the Sunday morning you mentioned, I was upstairs on the top floor, or what was left of it. Our men were having a very bad time – quite a lot of wounded. I was sent for by Col Stoney and found him in the basement. He said to me, "Crowe, you know the position?"

I replied, "I know and have studied it."

He said, "What do you think about it?"

I replied, "I'm not going to give in, I intend to fight it out or get out."

He said, "You're a married man and have children."

I said, "I know. I would like to try and get out."

He replied. "How many men do you want?"
I thought about 35 to make a show.

At this point, though Crowe does not mention it in his letter, the Reverend Tanner, who was listening to the conversation that day in 1918, recorded in his diary that the conversation continued as follows:

Crowe: "If we could knock out those machine guns over there, we will be able to make a run for it."
C.O: "Well Crowe, I'm not going to order you to do it but if you do, you'll be a very brave man.")

John James continues with his letter as follows:

I went upstairs and could only get 7 men, although a lot were lying about or watching through windows, which was a very dangerous thing to do. I came down and got the men together and told them what I was going to do. I wanted to get over to the cowshed (or it looked like that) where we should get a better view of the road outside. We made a dash for it and I could see one Boche about 50 yards away on our left. He saw me and I bolted back and tried to get a shot at him but he bolted back and I don't know whether I had hit but I did not see him again. On our right I could see a Boche machine-gun in action on the road having a shot at the Mairie. Looking at the road, I found that the gutters (drainage ditches) were deep so I placed 5 men facing the left watching the street where I saw the Boche. I told them to prevent any attack from the left. I noticed a lot of firing from our front from a bank and hedge. They were firing at the Marie but I don't think they saw us. So as there was no hope of a frontal attack I decided to crawl along the gutter to my right and try and get on to their flank. In this we were successful for about 150 yards and getting behind the bank we crawled up and then were able to enfilade the Boche. Three of us opened fire at them at about 100 yards. They were taken by surprise and started getting up and turning round. No one got away. I counted 23 killed or wounded. I took care that none of them was in a position to open fire on us. Then we heard a machine-gun firing down at the Mairie over the heads of the 23 out of action.

On crawling up the slope I could see that it was being fired by the Boche out of a shell hole. It was too dangerous to lie down in the open field and fire so we started to rush forward, firing at the hip to get a hit to prevent them shooting us up. As soon as we started, one of the two men with me was badly hit. Luckily, it was near a shell hole so we put him in it, hoping for the best. We continued to attack and killed two Boche. I don't know what happened to the third. He may have got into the hedge. I found one of our Lewis guns, which they had been using. We picked it up and started to return and then my other man was badly hit. There was nothing I could do for him so I could only get back myself. I was under fire from my right so I dropped down. I could see where the fire came from. I waited for about two minutes, jumped up and ran towards the home hedge but had to fall down again. They thought I was hit, so I waited till the firing stopped then I got up again and jumped into the hedge. Then out came the men I had left at the Mairie and picked me up and asked me if I was hurt. I told them I was alright and gave them the Lewis-gun to take to Col Stoney. I then reported to him and made it clear that we had to get out at once or be captured.

I started to lead them along the Dranoutre Road. Lieut Pointon did not go into the cowshed with the first lot but when I got back, he was out with the others. I cannot say what happened when we left the cowshed.

I am sorry to say that I did not know the names of the two men who went over the ridge with me. All I wanted was men in uniform. They were very brave and did not hesitate to help me out. You know how it was… no chance to make a note. We were staring death in the face. They were the bravest of the brave.

On our way out we were fired on by troops on the left hill but we could not say who they were. We stopped at a farm from which the owners had gone. Our lads killed a young pig and I had a taste of pork and was very glad to get anything to eat. After leaving the farm we found part of our Brigade.

I hope you will be able to make something out of this.
Yours sincerely
J Crowe.

The retirement from the Mairie was covered to the last by Private F. R Brough, who remained at a window, firing his Lewis-gun while the party got clear. This was a feat even more incredible when it is considered that the enemy's trench mortar fired at him constantly, eventually bringing down the roof behind him.

The small group of exhausted men staggered away as their retreat was protected by John James' detachment up on the hill. These men were the last to pull back and the enemy made no attempt to pursue them. As the men retired they passed through the lines of the Nottinghamshire and Derbyshire Regiment, who were unaware of what had happened at the Mairie and thought that it was they that were in the front lines.

2nd Battalion continued on their way, skirting around the village of Dranoutre, continuing on towards Locre. At around

6.30 that evening, the survivors of 2nd Battalion, consisting of just six officers and a hundred men – of whom approximately twenty-five were wounded, rejoined the rest of 100th Brigade behind Hill 70, near Hille. Here they discovered that the Brigade had given them up as lost and had no idea that they had managed to fight their way out. On Monday 15th, the gallant band were joined by a further few survivors who had also managed to escape and find their way back to the Battalion. It was a miracle that any of them made it back at all.

The 2nd, 3rd and 4th Battalions of the Worcestershire Regiment all found themselves in reserve positions on 15th April, trying to rest and recuperate amid the still incessant shellfire. Their rest, such as it was, was brief, as the front line south of Bailleul was attacked on the afternoon of the 15th in strength and the 49th West Riding Division, who were holding the line, was in danger of being over-run. Orders were sent for all troops behind the line to take up supporting positions, so that the Yorkshiremen could affect an ordered retreat.

Before long, the Worcestershire Battalions were deployed for action with 2nd Battalion taking up positions on the forward slope of Hill 70, 3rd Battalion were positioned north-east of Haegedoorne, while the 4th marched forward with the Brigade from Croix de Poperinghe to Hoogenacker, ready if required to deliver a counter-attack. That day, all three Battalions suffered heavy casualties.

Their job done, the Yorkshire Territorials passed back through the supporting positions, leaving 2nd and 3rd Battalions to hold the line. That evening, as the light dimmed, the enemy could be seen swarming down the slopes of the Ravelsberg and by the time it was dark they had come up against the Worcestershire's defensive line. All through the night the Worcestershires suffered in the cold and the rain, feverishly building up their defences for the attacks that the morning light would certainly bring.

Sure enough, at dawn on the 16th, the German's threw themselves at the British line. On the north side of the Ravelsberg the Germans surged forward, covered by intense artillery and machine gun fire. The British fought furiously as their Lewis guns glowed red-hot and with the aid of the French artillery, which had come up to support, the enemy's attack was repulsed. But despite their initial failure, the Germans attacked again and again, and eventually, at around 2.45pm they succeeded in overrunning the 10th Lincolns, who were immediately to the right of the 2nd Worcestershires. Holding their ground, and supporting a counter-attack by a company of the 9th Northumberland Fusiliers, again 2nd Battalion played a crucial role, helping to restore the status quo and stabilise the line.

On the 17th, the attacks were resumed, but this time with the aid of even greater numbers of German artillery pieces. This overwhelming shellfire blew the trenches in the centre of 100th Brigade's line to pieces. In this section of the line was an orchard, held by the Glasgow Highlanders, who were annihilated and the orchard duly fell. That afternoon counter-attacks, first by the Royal Scotts Fusiliers and then by two companies of the 5th York and Lancaster, failed to restore the situation, which was now becoming serious. The 2nd Worcestershire, on the left flank, continued to stand fast and gradually a new firing line on the outskirts of the orchard was established. By nightfall a continuous line had been deployed and the position was retaken.

At last, after a bitter struggle, 2nd Battalion was relieved by the West Riding Territorials who, restored to fighting strength, took over the line. By the 18th April, the remnants of 2nd Battalion had reached Westoutre and after a night's rest they rejoined with 100th Brigade, who along with the 33rd Division made their way to Mont des Cats. 2nd Battalion had paid a high price for the defence of the line and between 11th and 18th April 1918 the casualties suffered were as follows:

Officers killed (7); wounded (11); missing (6).
Other ranks killed (54); wounded (181); missing (274)

Altogether, the casualty toll amounted to 533 men and officers killed, wounded or missing. It was a heavy toll and between 20th April and the end of the month the Battalion spent time rebuilding its numbers. By the beginning of May, 2nd Battalion could muster some 600 men, but weeks of training were required in order to mould them into an effective fighting unit.

By the end of April 1918, the Battles of the Lys had come to an end. They had lasted for forty days and although the Germans had desperately tried to break through the British defences their efforts had proved unsuccessful and the channel ports were safe. As was often the case on the Western Front, the attacking side had fared far worse than the defending one and despite the fearful losses suffered by the British, the Germans had come off even worse. During those forty days and nights of fighting, that at times reached biblical proportions, the British had lost over 14,800 officers and 288,000 men killed, wounded, captured or missing, which amounted to more than a quarter of the British fighting troops under Sir Douglas Haig's command on 21st March 1918. The German losses, though, were even more appalling with

12,800 officers and 336,000 men lost. The staunch defence put up by the British during the Battles of the Lys is considered by many to be one of the finest achievements of the British Armies during the war. More importantly, the Germans could not afford to replace the men they had lost, the efforts of the Worcestershire Battalions and other elements of the British Army that stood and fought for those forty days went a long way towards actually winning the war. Research now shows that the 2nd Battalion moved from the mairie to the hospice before 11th April.

The Last Six Months of the War
May to November 1918.

Despite the travails of April 1918, the work that had been done to train the new recruits meant that the 33rd Division was in better shape than many other units, and so they were duly sent back to the line on 3rd May. The 2nd Battalion accordingly made their way by bus to Steenvoorde and by May 6th the Battalion was bivouacked near Poperinghe. The camp was in a small coppice and due to the proximity to the front; the troops were forced to lie under camouflaged screens, lest the enemy observers could see them from their positions on the formidable Kemmel Hill.

The weather that May was particularly cold and wet, causing influenza to become rife amongst the unseasoned troops. The situation wasn't helped by a German attack near Dickebusch on 8th May, which resulted in 2nd Battalion being brought forward from Poperinghe into divisional support near Busseboom. There they stayed for four days until French troops were moved up to hold the line, at which point 2nd Battalion were able to retire to a camp near Brandhoek.

As the German pushes fizzled out in the Ypres salient, gradually the area became quieter and as it did so reserve troops were able to move back to areas where training could be conducted with little interference from the German guns. On 24th May, 100th Brigade marched westward past Poperinghe once more and onto a camp beyond Watou. While there, on 29th May, the Corps Commander, Lieut General Sir Claud Jacob, K.C.B, inspected 2nd Battalion and wished them every success in their future operations. Three days before, John James Crowe had been formerly granted the rank of Acting Captain.

Come the 30th May, 100th Brigade marched eastwards once more to Dirty Bucket Camp, to the north-east of Poperinghe and replaced 19th Brigade in the forward area. 2nd Battalion remained there for a week before 33rd Division was moved up to the line to relieve the 71st Brigade, and the 2nd Worcestershire duly took over the reserve trenches near Belgian Chateau, allowing the 9th Norfolk to retire. During their stay, the Battalion spent their time improving the defences and at this time Lieut Colonel Stoney resumed command as Lieut Colonel Pardoe left the Battalion to take up a post in England. On 10th June, John James went to England on leave.

The German offensive during April had fallen hard on the Ypres Salient, reducing it in size and forcing the British back from the positions they had previously fought hard to win. The Germans now occupied the Passchendaele Ridge, the Messines Ridge and Mount Kemmel, meaning they could look down on the British positions around Ypres. The reduced size of the salient meant that even the British reserve positions were under constant and accurate bombardment, resulting in many casualties and a constant state of danger.

On the night of the 15th and 16th June, 2nd Worcestershire relieved the 1st Queen's in the front line southeast of Ypres along the shores of the Zillebeke Lake. Initially, things were quiet, allowing platoons to busy themselves repairing and improving defences. A raid was soon organised in order to identify the enemy formations holding the remains of Manor Farm, a strongly defended post that lay opposite the British positions.

The raid took place on the night of 19th and 20th June and consisted of five officers and 138 other ranks. At 12.15 am, they silently left their trenches and, creeping along the backs of the lake, they finally reached a German outpost in front of the ruined farm. Once in position they rushed it with bayonets fixed and all the defenders were captured or killed. The raiders then pushed forward towards the farm and attacked it, dropping a large explosive charge into a deep dugout nearby. The men then returned to the lines with five prisoners in tow. Thankfully, their own casualties were light, with only two of their number wounded and later that night the Battalion was relieved, allowing it to retire to the reserve. Total casualties for the Battalion during the period were five killed and forty-three wounded.

On 28th June 1918, John James's Victoria Cross was announced in the London Gazette. The citation read as follows:

For most conspicuous bravery, determination and skilful leading when the enemy, for the third time having attacked a post in a village, broke past on to the high ground and established a machine-gun and snipers in the broken ground at the back of the village. 2nd Lieut Crowe twice went forward with two NCOs and seven men to engage the enemy, both times in the face of active machine-gun fire and sniping.

His action was so daring that on each occasion the enemy withdrew from the high ground into the village, where 2nd Lieut Crowe followed them and himself opened fire upon the enemy as they collected in the doorways of the houses. On the second occasion, taking with him only two men of his party, he attacked two enemy machine-guns which were sweeping the post, killed both the gunners with his rifle and prevented any others from reaching the guns and bringing them in action again. He then turned upon a party of the enemy who were lined up in front of him, killed several and the remainder withdrew at once. He captured both guns, one of which was the Battalion Lewis gun, which had been captured by the enemy on the previous day.

Through seven days of operations, 2nd Lieut Crowe showed an utter disregard of danger and was recklessly brave. His personal example and cheerfulness contributed largely to the determination of the garrison of the post to hold out. It may surely be said that for his coolness and skill at the last moment, when he personally placed the covering party in close proximity to the enemy, who were again closing ground and were also forming up in fours near by, the garrison of the post could never have effected its escape.

The valour and zeal displayed by 2nd Lieut Crowe were of the highest order.

John James was 41 years old when he earned the highest award for valour and is believed to be the only man ever awarded the Victoria Cross who was already the holder of the Long Service and Good Conduct Medal.

On 30th June 1918, John James completed his 21st year of service in the Worcestershire Regiment and that same day 2nd Battalion moved forward again to relieve the 5th Scottish Rifles in the trenches they had previously held to the south of the canal. The next few days involved different units manoeuvring in and out of position and before long the Battalion found itself in positions at Scottish Wood.

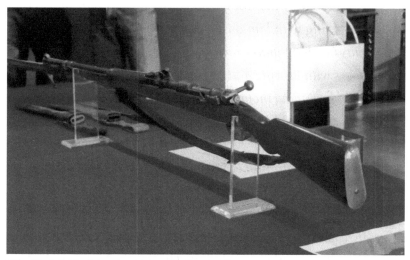

The Enfield Mk II, the type of rifle used by Captain Crowe V.C.

Before dawn on 9th July, a patrol lead by 2nd Lieut E. Morton-Hicks came across a German post in No Man's Land. To their amazement, they found the post empty and the small party returned with a light machine-gun and several overcoats. Further raids were conducted, one which involved the wounding of Lieut Scott and as a result of the actions the Battalion was forced to spend almost eighteen hours manning shell holes in No Man's Land. This sort of situation was common on the Western Front and often men found themselves manning parts of the line that consisted of little more than a string of shell holes. As the war entered into its final phase, and movement became more prevalent, these situations increased in frequency.

On 6th August 1918, King George V presented three Victoria Crosses at a ceremony at Blendecques. The recipients were:

Captain J. J Crowe, 2nd Battalion Worcestershire Regiment for his valour at Neuve Eglise in Belgium on 14th April 1918.

2nd Lieutenant C. L Knox, 150th Field Company Royal Engineers for his valour at Tugny in France on 22nd March 1918.

Sergeant C. W Train, 2/14th Battalion London Regiment (London Scottish) for his valour at Air Karim, near Jerusalem in Palestine on 8th December 1917.

During the course of the war very few Victoria Crosses were presented in the field and as a result it was considered an added honour to have them presented in this manner. Even so, some years later, John James commented to a reporter that he would rather have received his at Buckingham Palace, as it would have entailed a much needed seven days leave.

Following the presentations, His Majesty inspected a representative party from 100th Brigade, commanded by Captain E. O Underhill M.C. Later that week, on Sunday 11th August, another representative party, this time commanded by Captain C. C Trough M.C, paraded at a Divine Service attended by the King, and it was on this occasion that Reverend Tanner M.C was presented to the King.

As well as the Victoria Cross, John James was also awarded the Croix de Guerre avec Palme en Bronze, which was announced in the London Gazette on 17th August 1918. The Croix de Guerre was a French medal awarded for an individual feat of arms that had been mentioned in a French dispatch. The Palme en Bronze indicates that the despatch was from an Officer Commanding an Army and John James received his award at Festubert, a place he knew only too well.

King George V presenting Captain J. J Crowe with the Victoria Cross on 6th August 1918.

On 6th August 1918, King George V presented the Victoria Cross to Captain J.J Crowe, 2nd Lieut C. L Knox and Serg C. W Train at Blendecques, the Headquarters of the British Second Army.

2nd Battalion remained in the area south of Ypres holding alternate sections of the front and spending brief periods in the reserve until the middle of August. During this time, little of note occurred and as a result casualties remained light. This allowed the Battalion to become involved in training the raw American troops and by the middle of August the Americans were deemed to be competent enough to take over the line, accordingly the American 30th Division relieved the British 33rd. 2nd Battalion was relieved by a battalion from the American 120th Regiment and proceeded to retire behind the lines past Knollys Farm and on to Tunnellers Camp beyond Poperinghe. Here they rested for a further week before moving further back for a period of training.

In the autumn of 1918, William Crowe, John James' brother, who was serving with 4th Battalion Worcestershire Regiment, was wounded for the second time. His first wound had come while in the Dardenelles, although he had recovered sufficiently to retake his place with his unit. His second wound had come whilst in action in France, when he was shot in the wrist, thankfully, a minor wound. Even so, he was sent back to England to receive treatment at Reading War Hospital (subsequently known as Battle Hospital). On 25th October 1918, William left hospital and was discharged from the army. His war was over but his wound required further treatment over the coming months. He had completed a total of seven years and ninety-eight days with the Colours and was the recipient of both the Silver War Badge as well as the 1914-15 Star. He was also awarded the British War medal and the Victory Medal.

Meanwhile, back in France, 2nd Battalion was located amongst the shattered landscape of Delville Wood on the

Somme, the site where the South Africans had fought so gallantly during the Somme offensive of 1916. Here they trained with other elements of 100th Brigade before moving up past Les Boeufs, Le Transloy, Rocquigny until finally they reached Lechelle.

In front of them lay their next challenge and the roar of the guns told them that the battle along the Epehy Ridge, in which Third Army were already engaged and which they were soon to join, would be a further test of their resolve. The Germans, having learned the hard taught lessons from the Hindenberg Line in the previous year, had set out their defences in even greater depth than usual, strengthening their line with a heavily fortified 'forward zone' on the heights around Epehy and Gouzeacourt. These positions had to be taken and after the capture of these objectives 33rd Division was to pass through the forward lines and clear the long spurs that ran down from Epehy, by Ossus and Villers Guislain, then on to the St Quentin Canal.

19th Brigade had been tasked with the main attack and 2nd Battalion found themselves, on 20th September, ensconced in reserve trenches behind the main front of attack. The German defences arrayed in front of them were indeed formidable. Between the line at Epehy and the St Quentin canal, the forward defensive positions included two main lines of trenches, the second stronger than the first. This second line passed over the eastern ends of both Seventeen Spur, and Lark Spur and Pigeon Trench, which ran like a scar across the Targelle Valley, linked these two fortified positions. Nearly a mile west lay a deep sunken road named Gloster Road and some 200 yards west of this the enemy's first line of defence was located. This consisted of a trench fortified with elaborate redoubts; Limerick Post on the crest of Lark Spur and Meath Post about half a mile further to the north.

On 21st September, at dawn, the British artillery opened up with a rolling barrage and two Battalions of 19th Brigade, the 1st Cameronians and 1st Queens attacked both Limerick and Meath posts. Both attacks failed, but a further attack that evening by a battalion of the 5th Scottish Rifles succeeded in capturing Meath Post. To this point, 2nd Worcestershires had not been involved in the action, however orders soon arrived for them to relieve 1st Queens and renew the attack on Limerick Post.

At dawn on the 23rd, the British guns again opened fire and A and B Companies of 2nd Battalion advanced over the boggy ground, which had been soaked with rain the previous night. Despite heavy artillery fire, they reached Limerick Post and rushed the redoubt with bayonets fixed, only to find the defences abandoned, the enemy having fallen back during the night.

The rest of 100th Brigade was brought up and plans were made to pursue the attack. During the following four days, fighting raged along the spurs and valleys east of Epehy but despite the best efforts of the British, all these attacks were met with stiff resistance and all of them failed. From Cambrai southwards to St Quentin lay the most formidable array of defences on the Western Front, but they were defences that had to be broken. If a breakthrough was to occur then it would probably happen in the sector between Vendhuille and Bellicourt and as a result, the main resources of the British Army were concentrated to this end. American and Australian forces were directed to attack the tunnel defences at Bony and Bellicourt, while the British 46th Division, which was equipped with specialised bridging materials, would endeavour to cross the St Quentin Canal north of Bellenglise. Meanwhile, Third Army was to make a subsidiary attack from Epehy to Marcoing. On the right of this attack 33rd Division was to advance and take the German positions west of the canal. On the left flank, 33rd Division and 98th Brigade were to storm Villers Guislan. On the Division's right flank the 100th Brigade, including 2nd Worcestershire, were to attack down the Targelle Valley towards Ossus.

The attacks by the 33rd Division and 2nd Battalion were diversionary to the main thrust and so were to receive little in the way of artillery and tank support, so much so that Brigadier-General A. W. F Baird reported officially that there was little chance of success unless the attacks could be assisted by either tanks or increased artillery, or unless the enemy's machine-guns were effectively blinded by a heavy curtain of smoke. However, his pleas fell on deaf ears. The order stood.

At 5.30 am on 29th September, the British Guns behind 33rd Division thundered into life, signalling the start of the battle. The Worcestershire platoons advanced with all possible speed through a hail of German shells. The appalling weather of the preceding days had turned the battlefield to a quagmire and the troops were therefore unable to keep pace with their protective barrage. The results were predictably tragic and as the rolling barrage moved away down the valley, the German machine-guns swept the advancing British lines. Most were scythed down and the remainder sought cover wherever they could. By 10am it had been reported that the attacks had failed and under the cover of steadily falling mist the survivors returned to

Limerick Trench under a constant stream of German shells. As they reached the relative safety of their starting positions they heard the thunder of the main attacks going on along the whole Fourth Army's front.

The attack proved to be a major success and the diversionary attacks had not been in vain. The St Quentin Canal had been crossed and the Hindenburg line had been broken. This proved calamitous for the Germans and they retreated from all the positions along 33rd Division's front. Casualties from the previous day's fighting had been high; a total of 8 officers and 80 NCOs had been killed and 3 officers and 150 men had been wounded. No one had reached their objectives.

By nightfall on 9th October, the whole Hindenburg Line from Cambrai to St Quentin was in Allied hands and the Germans were in full retreat. Pursuit was given and by the following morning the British First, Third and Fourth Armies were advancing over open countryside. The stalemate of trench warfare had been broken and the war of movement had returned. The Allies were determined to push home their advantage.

During the closing weeks and months of the war, 2nd Worcestershire and the rest of 100th Brigade continued to play an active role as the Allies advanced all along the Western Front, until eventually, on 11th November, at 5.30am, the Armistice was signed at Rethondes railway station and at 11am that day the First World War formerly came to a close. That day, 2nd Battalion re-crossed the River Sambre and moved back to billets at Berlainmount. Four days later, 33rd Division concentrated further back and the 2nd Worcestershires made their way back through the forest of Mormal to the village of Englefontaine where they had been fighting three weeks before. The next day, the march was continued back along the line of the previous advance, down the main road through Forest then across the river Selle to billets in Clary, where the Battalion remained during the ensuing three weeks. As had happened at the beginning of the war, something that seemed a lifetime away, John James had been selected for other duties and he left 2nd Battalion bound for England, on 14th November 1918. Acting Captain John James Crowe V.C. was home at last. The war was finally over.

Chapter Four

John James Crowe's Last Army years December 1918 to November 1920

O N 30th November 1918, John James was posted to the 4th Reserve Battalion of the Northamptonshire Regiment. On the 3rd June, he relinquished his rank of Acting Captain and for the majority of 1919 he was the Adjutant at the Shorncliffe disembarkation Camp, near Folkestone in Kent. However, he did return to the Worcestershire Regiment to participate in the peace celebrations, which were held in Worcester in August 1919.

Shortly after the signing of the Treaty of Versailles, the Lord Lieutenant of Worcestershire announced plans for a parade of the County Forces in Worcester to celebrate the returning peace. The parade duly took place on 23rd August and it was the largest gathering of military forces seen in the city since 1887. Detachments from all Battalions of the Worcestershire Regiment were present and for the first time the Colours of all the four Regular Battalions were seen together on parade. Also represented were the Royal Navy, the County Yeomanry, the Territorial Artillery, the Volunteers, the W.A.A.Cs, the V.A.Ds, the Land Girls and several other women's organisations. Altogether there were a total of 10,148 men and 374 women on parade that day.

A long and detailed account of the day's ceremony appeared in Berrow's Worcestershire Journal on the following Saturday, 30th August 1919. One of the more poignant sections of that account is reproduced below:

Saluting the Cenotaph

The largest assembly of people was in the precincts of the cenotaph erected on the Cathedral Green. The scene here was deeply impressive. The completed cenotaph formed a simple and dignified memorial. It bore a Union jack and white and red ensigns and on the front a large laurel wreath, tied with a blood red ribbon – a reminder of the sacrifice so many had made. On each side stood, with reversed arms, the four gallant guards, Lt J Crowe V.C., Pte F Turrall V.C. (Both of the Worcestershire Regiment), Segt Wyatt V.C. (of Hindlip and the Coldstream Guards) and R.S.M Harwood D.C.M and bar (Rifle Brigade). At the base was a mass of rare blooms, the tributes of the relatives of the dead. Long before the procession arrived, widows, mothers and daughters came bearing wreaths and bunches of flowers which they laid on the base or on the ground adjacent to it. This laying down of flowers was a distressing ceremony to witness. Some of the bereaved people could not restrain their grief, which the sight of the monument stirred. Most pathetic sight of all was the number of widows with young children. Several of them (little mites of only a few years of age) deposited posies of flowers. One mother or widow (one could not really tell which) placed a tiny bunch of jasmine. Another widow, with admirable self-preservation, walked up with a perambulator and two children. She placed a wreath among the tributes and withdrew. Quite obviously it was an ordeal for her but she maintained her composure. Among the tributes was one from the mayor and Corporation composed mostly of scarlet flowers and bearing the words 'In this sign they conquered and still live". There were also wreaths from the officers and non-commissioned officers and men of each of the Battalions – 1st to 4th of the Worcestershire Regiment, "In memory of our fallen comrades". Another was "To the heroes of the 8th Battalion" from Colonel and Mrs A Webb. The officers, non-commissioned officers and men of the Depot sent 'A tribute to the memory of all the officers, non-commissioned officers and men of the Worcestershire Regiment who gave their lives in the Great War". A great laurel wreath, with white lilies, formed "The women's tribute".

Over nine thousand soldiers of all ranks had given their lives for their King and Country while serving with the twelve fighting Battalions of the Worcestershire Regiment during the First World War.

On 1st October 1919, John James was formerly promoted to Captain and in 1920, he spent a brief spell of duty in Dublin with the Worcestershire Regiment, where he was involved in the arrest of Michael O'Connor, one of the prominent Sinn Fein leaders.

On Saturday 26th June 1920, Their Majesties King George V and Queen Mary invited recipients of the Victoria Cross to a reception at Buckingham Palace. The garden party took place between 4 and 6 o'clock in the afternoon. John James, his wife

Margaret and their elder daughter, Annie, were among the guests. During the course of the afternoon there was a sudden downpour and Annie, wearing her best dress, dashed into the nearest shelter, only to find that she had actually gone into the Royal tent. Annie's concern at her predicament was evident from her expression, however Queen Mary came to her rescue. The Queen placed a hand on Anne's shoulder and said, "Don't worry my dear, you can stay here until the rain stops."

At his own request, John James retired from the army on 22nd November 1920 in order to take up a new career in civilian life. He transferred to the Reserve of Officers, in which he remained until his 50th birthday. A number of senior officers in the Worcestershire Regiment provided John James with testimonials and one typical of these, provided by Lieut Colonel Chichester, is reproduced below:

I have the greatest pleasure in giving a testimonial to Capt J. J Crowe, V.C., late of the Worcestershire Regiment. I have served many years in the Worcestershire Regiment with him and therefore know him intimately and can speak from personal experience of his work. He has passed from Private to Captain during a period of about 23 years service without any blemish on his character. He served in the 3rd Battalion prior to the war with the rank of Colour Sergeant for many years. He was a very intelligent, active and keen soldier and a strict teetotaller. He was a great musketry expert, a first-rate sportsman and athlete. In each of these he showed everyone in the Battalion a splendid example.

What he excelled at in peacetime stood him in good stead at war. He soon got his chance and took it gaining the Victoria Cross for gallantry. I don't think anyone was in the least bit surprised. I certainly was not.

Captain Crowe is a very exceptional man. His moral and physical character was of a very high order and I know the Regiment is proud of having produced such a fine soldier.

(Signed) W. R Chichester.

Lieut Colonel.

The Worcestershire Regiment.

Chapter Five

After the Army

B ETWEEN 1921 and 1946, John James Crowe V.C. was the Children's Care Officer for the Brighton Education Committee. There were over two hundred applicants for the post and no doubt the military and personal record of John James helped him to secure the post.

Socially, members of the committee found Captain Crowe to be a very likeable colleague who was always happy to take part in many office and sporting activities, including being a member of the Education Committee cricket team, something that belied his true age.

British Legion dinner, Woodington Branch.

As part of his duties, John James would visit the parents of children absent from school. When families needed help, which they often did in those hard times, he did his best to provide it and he always carried out his duties quietly and efficiently without any mention of his war experiences.

On his retirement, John James became a prominent member of the Royal British Legion and he helped with their fund raising for many years. Another of his interests was the Woodingdean Happy Circle Club, of which he was president and a member for sixteen years. He was also a member of the Woodingdean Horticultural Society and always exhibited his flowers and vegetables with a great care to detail.

John James was also a great lover of animals and earlier in his life he had owned dogs; first spaniels and then a mongrel called Binty. Unfortunately, Binty was involved in an accident in which one of his legs was badly hurt and John James nursed the animal back to health. Towards the end of his life, John James also was the proud owner of two budgies.

John James remained active on retirement and enjoyed spending time with his grandchildren. In 1957, his Granddaughter, Doreen, attended a concert at the Dome in Brighton given by the renowned organist Douglas Reeve

Granddad in his front garden.

John Crowe meeting his great granddaughter for the first time in 1959.

with her Grandfather and his friends from the Happy Circle.

His fame, like so many Victoria Cross winners, often preceded him, something that was apparent in March 1964 when he attended a screening of the film Zulu. Nigel Green, the actor who played the role of the Colour Sergeant Major in the film, appeared on stage with John James and Mrs Elizabeth Chamberlain, whose grandfather had served with the South Wales Borderers at the Battle of Rorkes Drift and survived, to much applause.

John Crowe at a civic reception in 1962.

Throughout John James' life he always took great pleasure from his family and friends. He was a man who enjoyed helping others and sharing his knowledge with them. Despite his intelligence, bravery and sense of responsibility, he always enjoyed the simple pleasures of life, something that undoubtedly helped him to cope during the darkest days of the First World War.

Chapter Six

Epilogue

JOHN JAMES CROWE died on 27th February 1965 at Brighton General Hospital. His funeral was due to take place at the Church of the Holy Cross in Woodingdean, but as the roads were impassable due to snow and ice, this had to be abandoned. Instead, the service was held at Downs Crematorium in Brighton, albeit forty minutes late due to the weather.

Reverend R. D Patterson, the vicar of the Church of the Holy Cross, walked from Woodingdean to conduct the service, as too did A. J Patching and Mr A Bootman, who represented the Royal British Legion, and Mr Arch Smith, Chairman of the Woodingdean Happy Circle Club. Captain T. T Holland, who had travelled by train from Arundel in Sussex, represented the Worcestershire Regiment. Captain Holland accompanied the Reverend E. V Tanner of Weymouth, the same Reverend who had witnessed John James agreeing to take on the mission in which he won his Victoria Cross.

During the service the coffin was draped with the Union Jack and Reverend Tanner recounted the events that had lead up to John James winning his medal. Two officers and a bugler

Dedication of garden seat.

Plaque unveiling.

from the Worcestershire Regiment arrived just as the funeral procession left the crematorium, just too late to play the Last Post. After his death, a garden seat at the Community Hall in Woodingdean was dedicated to John James' memory during a brief ceremony in which his daughter, Anne, said a few heartfelt words.

Several years later, on 16th April 2011, the Last Post was played in honour of Captain John James Crowe V.C. after the unveiling of a memorial plaque. A fitting tribute and one of which no doubt John James would have approved.

Chapter 7

The unveiling of the Captain John James Crowe V.C. memorial plaque

THERE WERE many people at De Bosgeus (the former hospice) in Nieuwkerke that day. Major John Cotterill MBE, accompanied by two officers of the Mercian Regiment, was in attendance, as were the Belgian dignitaries, Burgermaster Bernard Heens and Culture Minister Gunter Perry. Also in attendance were representatives of the British Torch of Remembrance and the Royal British Legion, members of the Ramsgate 1957 and Dover 1900 Rifle Club, a local band and two members of the Menin Gate buglers. No less than thirty members of the Crowe family were also present, some having travelled from as far afield as Canada and Germany and they were all welcomed by the owner of De Bosgeus, who remarked that it was a great honour to have the plaque mounted on his wall.

During the ceremony, the Belgian dignitaries gave speeches that warmly conveyed not only their appreciation for their liberators but also their eternal respect and honour for those

The Last Post was played by two of the Menin Gate buglers for Captain J. J Crowe V.C on 16th April 2011.

that fell during the conflict. Billy Hollis, secretary of the Ramsgate 1957 and Dover 1900 Rifle Club, also gave a moving speech. In it he detailed how during December 2008, along with Major John Cotterill MBE and other members of the rifle club, he had visited Nieuwkerke. Walking around in the bitterly cold weather, they saw a plaque to the memory of Frederick Dancox V.C. and as Captain J.J. Crowe V.C. was a member of their club between 1908 and 1911 they determined that there should be a memorial to Captain Crowe, too. In search of John James' relatives, Billy contacted a family researcher who was able to track down my sister Andrea and myself.

Major John Cotterill MBE spoke on behalf of his regiment, describing the honour that he and the regiment felt because J.J Crowe V.C. was one of theirs. Major Cotterill said that he was often asked why there was a need for rifle clubs, at which point he would tell those that enquired of Captain John James Crowe

Major John Cotterill giving his speech on 16th April 2011 at Nieuwkerke in Belgium.

Doreen Pannett, the elder granddaughter of J. J Crowe V.C, giving her speech at Niewkerke in Belgium on 16th April 2011.

V.C.'s competition shooting at Bisley and how his outstanding marksmanship had almost certainly saved his life and that of his entire Battalion.

Major Cotterill then introduced Captain Crowe's grand-daughter, Doreen Pannett, remarking how similar she looked to her grandfather. The main part of her speech is reproduced below:

I knew John James Crowe quite well and I want to tell you about him, though of course I and my sister called him 'Granddad'.

Granddad was about fifty-six when I was born and he lived a few miles from us in the village of Woodingdean, on the south coast near Brighton. Granddad remained close to us and saw both my sister and I grow up, following our careers and attending our weddings.

Despite his age (sixty-two) at the outbreak of the Second World War he was disappointed not to be able to 'do his bit' in active service. After my father was taken Prisoner of War, Granddad helped to raise money for the Red Cross parcels. He also encouraged us to give concerts and I remember singing 'Alice blue gown'. I remember how he also sold his vegetables to raise money and how on his weekly visits he always brought some round for us, sometimes with a duck egg or a rabbit he had caught. When I started playing hockey it was Granddad who taught me how to use my wrists when holding a hockey stick in order to control the ball.

Many years later, my husband, Robin, took a photo of a young Queen Elizabeth II who was on a royal visit to Ghana on the royal yacht Britannia. The photo showed an army band dressed in red jackets on parade. Granddad inspected the photo carefully, nodding his approval, 'just like my regiment', he said. As I watched him, I could see the memories flooding back for him.

We, the Crowe family, are delighted that Granddad's bravery has been remembered. My sister, Andrea Tingey, recalled Granddad's favourite phrase, which was 'Loverly, tell your mum'.

Granddad was a committee member of the Woodingdean branch of the Royal British Legion. He was also on the committee of the Happy Circle. Andrea sometimes went with him to the Happy Circle meetings. Granddad made buttonhole posies for the ladies using flowers from his garden. The ladies all thought she was very lucky to have a grandad like him.

My mother's cousin, Fran Crowe (aged eighty-nine), spoke about his visits to us at Portslade during the Second World War. He and his uncle, Captain J.J Crowe V.C., used to go riding on the South Downs on John James' motorbike and sidecar, often returning with a rabbit or two.

After the speeches, we went outside and stood in front of the memorial plaque, which was covered with a Union Jack. I said, 'It is an honour and privilege to be here today to unveil this plaque in memory of my grandfather, Captain John James

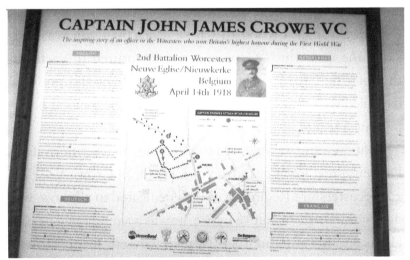

The plaque dedicated to the memory of Captain J. J Crowe V.C.

Crowe V.C., a soldier devoted to his country and his regiment'. I then pulled a cord and the Union Jack fell to the side. The plaque had a photo of Captain John James Crowe V.C., a map of the route he took and the citations in English, French, Flemish and German.

The Reverend Brian Llewellyn, Chaplain of St. George's Memorial Church, Ypes, then dedicated the plaque and prayers were said. Two of the Menin Gate buglers then played the Last Post and the flags of the Royal British Legion were lowered before two minutes silence was observed. During these minutes of reflection, wreaths were laid, first by my sister Andrea and then by the president of the Royal British Legion. The Reveille was sounded and banners were raised before a local band played the Belgian and British national anthems.

In the afternoon, we had a walk through Nieukerke, lead by Major Cotterill MBE, who told us about the battle of Neuve Eglise. We started at the churchyard and as I looked at the open countryside and rolling hills in the distance, we were told about the enemy advance. We saw the brewery and the town hall before returning to the former hospice. We then climbed the hill through a wood to where a machine gun was once sited, the one which Captain Crowe captured to earn him the Victoria Cross. It was a poignant moment and my voice trembled with emotion as the heroic story I had heard before became a reality.

That evening, we attended the Menin Gate ceremony. Luke Pannett, great great grandson of Captain J.J Crowe V.C., laid a Worcestershire Regiment wreath dedicated to all those who died at the Battle of Neuve Eglise, he was accompanied by Billy Hollis and his grandmother, Doreen Pannett. It was a fitting end to a very moving and memorable day.

Appendix I
Army Career Captain John James Crowe, V.C.

January 1912 – August 1914
Colour Sergeant with the 3rd Battalion Worcester Regiment based at Tidworth.
1st October1913 – Promoted to Company Sergeant Major.
5th August 1914 – Promoted to Quarter Master Sergeant.

6th August 1914 – September 1917
Q.M.S at No 29 Infantry Base B.E.F Depot, Rouen, France.
Awarded 1914 Star with bar – This medal implies that John James came under enemy fire some time between August and November 1914.
15th January 1915 – Promoted to Warrant Officer Class II.

6th September 1917 – March 1918
Promoted to Regimental Sergeant Major.
Mentioned in Earl Haig's despatch from France dated
7th April 1918 (for his activities during the period 25th September 1917 – 24th February 1918) and printed in the London Gazette on 23rd May 1918.

18th March – 14th November 1918
Appointed to a permanent Commission as 2nd Lieut and posted to 2nd Battalion.
11th to 14th April 1918 – As Acting Captain and Acting Adjutant was engaged in the defence of Neuve Eglise, during which, on April 14th he won the Victoria Cross.

26th May 1918 – Appointed to Acting Captain.

10th June 1918 – Proceeded on leave to the U.K

6th August 1918 – Victoria Cross presented by the King at Blendecques, France.

- Awarded Croix de Guerre. Printed in the London Gazette 17th August 1918.

14th November 1918 – Left France and returned to the U.K.

30th November 1918 – 22nd November 1920

Posted to 4th Reserve Battalion Northamptonshire Regiment.

1919 – Adjutant at the disembarkation camp at Folkestone.

24th February 1919 – Special employment by the War Office.

3rd June 1919 – Relinquished rank of Acting Captain.

23rd August 1919 – Participated in the Victory Parade at Worcester.

1st October 1919 – Promoted to Captain.

1920 – Served with the Worcestershire Regiment in Ireland.

22nd November 1920 – Retired from the army and transferred to the Reserve of Officers.

Appendix II
Details of medals (from left to right)

Medals, left to right.

Victoria Cross – The citation announcing the award was published in the London Gazette on 28th June 1918.

1914 Star and bar – Awarded to officers and men of the British Expeditionary Force who served in France or Belgium on the establishment of a unit between 5th August and 22nd November 1914.

British War Medal – Awarded to those that served in the First World War.

Victory Medal 1918 with Leaf – Awarded to those that served in the war. The leaf denotes a mention in despatches.

King George VI Coronation Medal – Presented on 12th May 1937.

Queen Elizabeth II Coronation Medal – Presented 2nd June 1953.

Long Service and Good Conduct Medal

French Croix de Guerre avec Palm en Bronze

As detailed in *Supplement to the London Gazette 25 June 1918* (7618)

2nd Lt. John Crowe, Wore. R.

For most conspicuous bravery, determination, .and skilful leading when the enemy, for the third time having attacked a post in a village, broke past on to the high ground and established a machine gun and snipers in the broken ground at the back of the village. 2nd Lt. Crowe twice went forward with two N.C.Os. and seven men to engage the enemy, both times in face of active machine-gun fire and sniping. His action was so daring that on each occasion the enemy withdrew from the high ground into the village, where 2nd Lt. Crowe followed them and himself opened fire upon the enemy as they collected in the doorways of the houses.

On the second occasion, taking with him only two men of his party, he attacked two enemy machine guns which were sweeping the post, killed both the gunners with his rifle, and prevented any others from reaching the guns and bringing them in action again. He then turned-upon a party of the enemy who were, lined up in front of him, killed several, and the remainder withdrew at once. He captured both the guns, one of which was the battalion Lewis gun which had been captured by the enemy on the previous day.

Throughout the seven days of operations 2nd Lt. Crowe showed an utter disregard of danger and was recklessly brave. His personal example and cheerfulness contributed largely to the determination of the garrison of the post to hold out: It may safely be said that but for his coolness and skill at the last moment, when he personally placed the covering party in close proximity to the enemy, who were again closing round, and were also forming up in fours nearby, the garrison of the post could never have effected its escape. The valour and zeal displayed by 2nd Lt. Crowe were of the highest order.

Appendix III
Rifle Shooting Competitions

1904 and 1905 – Sweetenham Cup and Inter-colonial Rifle Cup.

1903 and 1909 – Inter-Colonial Challenge Cup (Fired at Lydd and won by 3rd Battalion).

1910, 1911 and 1912 – John Crowe won the Shooting Cup at the Dover Rifle Club.

1910 – Queen's Cup (Society of Miniature Rifle Clubs).

1903, 1904, 1905 and 1913 – Queen Victoria Cup (3rd Battalion Worcestershire Regiment).

1913 – Roberts Cup (Won by 3rd Battalion). *This was the last ever presented by Field Marshall Lord Roberts of Kandahar at the Bisley meeting.*

1913 – Inter-Regimental Cup, Southern Command (Won by Tidworth).

1913 – Sergeant's Cup (Salisbury Plain District Rifle meeting).

Appendix IV

A selection of events attended by John James Crowe V.C.

9th November 1929

Inaugural V.C. Dinner in the Royal Gallery of the House of Lords

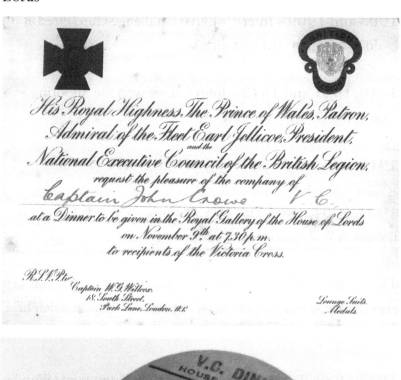

26th June 1956

Hyde Park. Review of Holders of the Victoria Cross

27th June 1956

Reception at Guildhall to mark the centenary of the Institution of he Victoria Cross

31st October 1964

The Cathedral Church of Christ and the Blessed Virgin Mary in Worcester. A form of thanksgiving to commemorate the 50th anniversary of the Battle of Cheluvelt, fought in Belgium on the 31st October, 1914.

Appendix V
Official History

100th Brigade.

33rd Division.

2nd BATTALION

WORCESTERSHIRE REGIMENT

APRIL 1918.

Report on Operations attached.

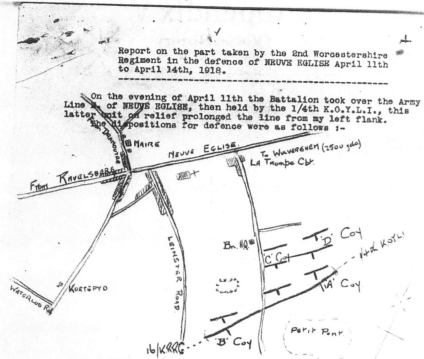

Report on the part taken by the 2nd Worcestershire Regiment in the defence of NEUVE EGLISE April 11th to April 14th, 1918.

On the evening of April 11th the Battalion took over the Army Line of NEUVE EGLISE, then held by the 1/4th K.O.Y.L.I., this latter unit on relief prolonged the line from my left flank. The dispositions for defence were as follows :-

A and B Companies in the front line with D and C Companies in close support to them respectively.

As it appeared clear that my left flank was the most threatened I withdrew C Company to a position of Reserve and ordered it to dig in along the lane which crossed the LA TROMPE CBT. - PETIT PONT RD., close to Battalion H.Qs. (which was in a cement dugout there).

By daylight on the 12th this Company was well dug in and screened from view by the hedge which ran along the lane.

At dawn on April 12th, acting on instructions from Brigade I pushed out two strong patrols (25 and a Lewis Gun), each under an Officer (2nd Lts. NICKLIN and PARRY), their orders were to go out beyond the Army Line and locate and engage the enemy, the object being to deceive the latter as to our rear line of defence. These patrols almost immediately got into touch with superior forces of Germans whom they engaged and held at bay inflicting heavy losses upon them, and it was not till later in the day when, owing to heavy hostile shelling and enveloping pressure by increased enemy numbers and Machine Guns, were these patrols forced to withdraw to our lines. They rendered a most splendid service by thus considerably delaying the pending enemy attack.

Throughout the 12th a continuous stream of small parties of Germans could be seen, with the naked eye, moving in a S. direction from MESSINES RIDGE towards PLOEGSTEERT WOOD. German artillery also came into action in full view of our positions and opened fire at almost point blank range.

Whilst this irregular movement was taking place across our front small parties of enemy trickled across the country towards our line sometimes coming clearly into view, and then disappearing again in the folds of the ground and behind hedges. They kept no formation. Some wore equipment and packs, others did not. Some mounted men also were seen moving amongst these parties of Germans.

Fire was not opened from the Army Line at this period, as the enemy were not close enough and the intention then was to conceal our real line of defence, our advanced patrols however, engaged these parties of the enemy.

A hostile 'plane came over during the morning and locating our advanced patrols, dropped lights, whereupon the latter were almost immediately shelled by German artillery.

Considerable movement developed along the whole Brigade Sector about mid-day. Enemy M.G's seemed to increase in number and their fire was very active being directed all over our position.

I was not quite satisfied as regards my right flank and foreseeing the possibility of an attack from this point upon the village, sent a platoon from C Company (Reserve) to occupy the further hedge of the enclosure immediately in support of B Company (front right).

Towards evening enemy activity showed a marked increase along the whole Brigade Sector, the village was heavily shelled throughout, also very heavy M.G. fire.

At about 7.30 p.m. the 1/4th K.O.Y.L.I. were attacked and a part of the enemy approached my left, but were easily driven off.

The dispositions of the Battalion were as follows :-
(7.30 p.m. 12th April).-

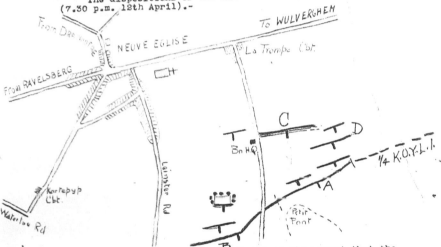

Almost at the same time I received the report that the 16th K.R.R.C., on my immediate right had been attacked and their line broken, so I immediately ordered C Company (Reserve) to form a defensive flank across this portion of NEUVE EGLISE which appeared to be in danger.

The positions to which C Company was directed were as follows:-

- 3 -

Information being received that the line held by the K.R.R.C. Had been re-established the above dispositions were not made until the following morning, (13th).

During the night Battalion H.Qs. moved to the Brewery, here I was more centrally placed and in close touch with the units on my flanks, moreover, LA TROMPE CBT. - PETIT PONT RD. was under direct observation by the enemy, where all movement had to be done under direct M.G.fire.

Early on the morning of the 12th the enemy broke through the K.R.R.C., reached the village and got past the Brewery and my H.Qs. 2nd Lieut. Pointon collected all available men at H.Qs., rushed to the cross roads W. of the Church, at the same time I ordered C Company to immediately counter-attack the enemy and occupy those positions I had indicated on the previous evening. This counter-attack was carried out promptly and thoroughly, with the result that the enemy's stay in the village was short, for withdrawing down the LEINSTER RD. he was caught between our counter-attack and a party of the Hallamshire Rgt., who were then coming up. All these Germans were accounted for, some 60 being killed and about 20 taken prisoner, besides about 6 machine guns, these latter were destroyed as it was not possible then to get them away.

The dispositions of the Battalion were now as follows :- (mid-day April 13th).-

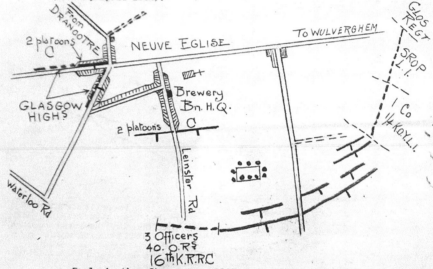

Early in the afternoon an Officer of the Glasgow Highlanders and two platoons reported to me at the Brewery and asked for instructions. I therefore ordered him to prolong the right of my Reserve Coy. (C) then thrown across LEINSTER RD., and to endeavour to obtain touch with a party of his own Battalion, believed to be on the NEUVE EGLISE-KORTEPYP CABT. RD. A portion of my Reserve Coy. were then in touch with some Glasgow Highlanders on the NEUVE EGLISE - RAVELSBERG RD.

Until about mid-day I had been in telephonic communication with the O.C., Glasgow Highlanders, but this had now ceased. During the afternoon I ordered the following dispositions :-

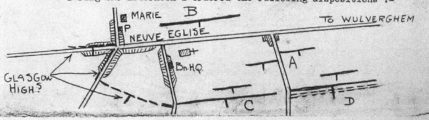

That portion of C Company then holding the cross roads of the village and were in touch with the Glasgow Highlanders on the RAVELSBERG – NEUVE EGLISE RD., was to rejoin its Company at LEINSTER RD. at dusk, when the above dispositions would be made.

I considered this alteration of my line necessary in view of the fact that my right flank was now almost completely in the air and the unit on my left, had, with the exception of one Company, withdrawn from the Army Line, and that one still remaining had thrown back across the NEUVE EGLISE – WULVERGHEM RD.

B Company was to move to the N. side of the village by the Church and be in Battalion Reserve.

These above moves by Companies were to be carried out with the greatest caution, one party covering the other's withdrawal with fire.

At about 6 p.m. I received a message from O.C., A Company, saying that the enemy were attacking in strength and that if his line was not to be broken it was necessary to carry out the new arrangement immediately. I therefore ordered my front Companies to immediately withdraw fighting, to their new positions.

At 6.30 p.m. I moved Battalion H.Qs. to the MAIRIE and at once decided to hold it as a strong point, and issued instructions for its defence as follows :-

2 platoons were to be held as final reserve in the cellars,
1 platoon in addition to H.Qs. personnel were to defend the building.
1 platoon to occupy the house marked P.

Lewis Guns were to be placed in position on the ground floor behind windows and to cover the ground E. of the MAIRIE and also the main roads of the village and Church area.

3 riflemen were to man each window.

A M.G. which had just reported to me, was ordered to assist the Lewis Guns.

The platoon allotted to the house marked P. was to hold the road and generally act as a buffer to the MAIRIE.

At about 8 p.m. the O.C., B Company arrived at the MAIRIE with only two platoons, he reported to me that on the request from Os.C., A and D Companies, he had sent a platoon to each of them as they were being very hard pressed by the enemy whilst carrying out the re-arrangement of their line. There was now very heavy M.G. and rifle fire all along the village and a good deal of shelling over the village.

It was impossible now for two platoons to be held as a final reserve, so half a platoon was placed in the house marked P. and a large supply of bombs were issued (this house was about 40 yards in front of the MAIRIE). The remaining one and a half platoons and Battalion HQs. manned the MAIRIE.

Reliefs were arranged so that a certain number of fresh men were ready to relieve those on duty. A large supply of bombs was found and they were issued out.

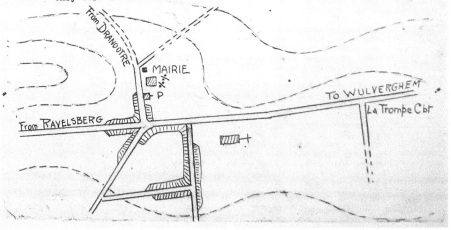

Runners who were sent forward to the front line Companies to ascertain the situation there and to report the position of the new Battalion H.Qs., did not return.

Almost as soon as it was dark a very light was fired about 80 yards distant from the MAIRIE and in line with the Church, this was followed a few minutes later by more very lights, by the light of which a party of about 12 Germans were detected moving round the left of the building. Our M.G. immediately opened fire, whereupon the Germans withdrew leaving one dead on the ground. Shortly after this a very sharp M.G. fire was directed on to our M.G. putting it out of action.

Much activity was noticed at the cross roads of the village from which point very heavy M.G. fire was directed down the DRANOUTRE RD. in the direction of the MAIRIE, numerous very lights were fired from the high ground on the right.

A motor machine gunner also had reported at Battalion H.Qs. earlier in the evening, engaged the enemy M.G. at the cross roads, when a lively duel kept up for a considerable time until the motor Machine gunner was wounded.

Attempts were then made to silence the M.G. at the cross roads by means of rifle grenades fired from the garden in front of the MAIRIE. This met with success, for the M.G. fire down the road now ceased, but heavy fire from the direction of the Church still continued.

At about 1 a.m. movement was heard on the road which ran past the MAIRIE and a party of Germans were seen to be approaching from the rear of the building, the sentries at once opened fire and the Germans cleared off leaving one, a Company Sgt. Major, lying on the road, this man very severely wounded was taken into the Aid Post and interrogated.

The situation had become somewhat quieter, but towards morning the garrison of house P was forced to withdraw to the MAIRIE owing to heavy M.G. fire and bombs, which made communication between them and H.Qs. most difficulty.

A bomb was thrown from the rear of the MAIRIE and actually fell into one of the cellars, through the window which faced our rear, causing two casualties.

It was a very dark night making it extremely difficult to see exactly what was happening, and to obtain reports from the Companies was now impossible, for those runners sent out did not return, the enemy appeared to have managed to get almost completely round our position.

The greatest vigilance had to be maintained from all quarters of the MAIRIE. As soon as it became sufficiently light, the enemy was seen to be occupying the village in strength, movement could be observed in almost every house and also in the open ground by the Church. Lewis gun and rifle fire was at once opened on all hostile parties.

Trench Mortar shells began to fall about the MAIRIE, several direct hits being obtained two burst inside the rooms causing many casualties. M.G. fire increased from the direction of the Church, the cross roads and also the high ground on our right, whilst small groups of Germans were seen to rush forward. Sniping was directed upon our back windows and doors from the outhouses.

At about 8 a.m. we were absolutely surrounded and it was clear that a determined assault was imminent.

2nd Lt. Johnson begged permission to try and get through to the Brigade, giving him the situation, verbally, I very reluctantly consented to his request. This very gallant Officer has not since been heard of.

A further attempt was made to communicate with our troops on the left, though it was not known where they were, one of two runners who attempted to cross from the outhouses to the lane in rear, was shot the instant he emerged from the building, the other had to come back.

Every/

Every effort was now directed towards checking the enemy's further approach, so a lewis gun was mounted in one of the top windows of the MAIRIE and every available sniper was posted in position of observation. 2nd Lt. Turley directed rifle grenade fire into the outhouses and also on to the road and adjacent houses. This combined action soon took effect, for the sniping from the rear ceased and the enemy were noticed clearing out of the houses near P. But he still maintained his hold on the high ground on our right and also the Church area; certain it was, however, that a way to our rear must be kept open, otherwise our position would very soon become untenable.

2nd Lt. Crowe therefore volunteered to take a small party with a view to clearing the enemy from our rear, this very gallant Officer met with considerable success for on reaching the road a hostile party with M.G. was encountered and driven off on to the high ground. Leaving 2 N.C.O's and 5 men here to guard the road, 2nd Lt. Crowe went forward with only 2 men in order to work round the outer flank of their party, which he succeeded in doing, and by opening rapid fire in co-operation with those he had left on the road under 2nd Lt. Pointon, forced the Germans to withdraw still further up the hill.

By a determined and quick forward movement now by both 2nd Lts. Crowe and Pointon, the latter having being reinforced from the MAIRIE the enemy was pushed back to the line of the houses leaving many dead on the ground and 3 machine guns captured.

A line of defence was now established close to the crest of the high ground and a strong post on the road maintaining communication with Battalion H.Qs.

During the above described very daring and energetic sortie on the part of 2nd Lts. Crowe and Pointon, hot fire was kept up from the defenders of the MAIRIE, fire being directed onto the houses and the cross roads, where the Germans offered a fine target.

The Germans now were seen to be withdrawing by small groups to the centre of the village, this opportunity I at once seized of once again trying to get in touch with units on either flank, runners were therefore sent with messages requesting the O.C's, the units concerned to co-operate in a combined and converging attack upon the centre of NEUVE EGLISE.

I received a reply from the O.C., unit on my left, who had moved back to the N. of NEUVE EGLISE, saying that he would do all he could, but no reply came from my right.

An Officer from the VIII Corps School Bn. came to my H.Qs. during this lull (about 11 a.m.) and stated that he had been ordered forward with a party to reconnoitre the situation. I gave him a letter to "O.C., troops DRANOUTRE" stating the situation, and requesting that a Battalion if possible be sent up without delay, and that if the O.C. would report to me I would direct him: this I considered most urgent if the village of NEUVE EGLISE was to be saved.

At about 1 p.m. what appeared to be a party of Highlanders was seen moving through the village from the rear of the Church and towards LEINSTER RD. I therefore concluded that the assistance I had asked for from my flanks was actually being effected. But this almost as quickly proved to be a delusion, for a few minutes later Germans were seen forming up in the street by the brewery.

Coinciding with this the bombardment of the MAIRIE by trench mortars re-opened, also M.G. and rifle fire was again directed from the high ground on the right and also the Church - several casualties occurred in the MAIRIE.

By the numbers of the enemy in the village and the activity of his M.G's on our flanks, it was clear that another and more violent attack on the MAIRIE was determined. From the top windows the German troops were to be seen moving up in fours. (1.30 p.m.).

The covering party was still in position on the hill, but these men could not maintain their ground if attacked in any force.

2t/

It was impossible to reinforce them as all forward movement came under close M.G. fire.

The troops from DRANOUTRE which I had hoped to see had not turned up and I knew that if the enemy again succeded in surrounding the MAIRIE all our communications would be finally closed.

I therefore came to the decision that our position had to be given up in order to save Battalion H.Qs. and to regain touch with those of our troops on either flank.

At 1.45 p.m. I ordered all in the MAIRIE to evacuate. 2nd Lt. Crowe made his way to our men in position on the hill and the post on the road, instructing them to cover the withdrawal of the remainder.

The withdrawal of the entire garrison and also the covering party was effected without loss, in spite of a very heavy and continuous enemy M.G. fire which continued to sweep the slopes of the ground until the railway line was reached. 3 of our wounded who could not be moved, were left behind in the cellars of the MAIRIE, their wounds previously being dressed.

Withdrawing across the railway we passed through positions in rear held by our troops. 2nd Lt. Pointon who had moved towards the DRANOUTRE RD. was fired upon by British sentries who thought we were hostile troops.

Early on the morning of 14th runners who had been sent out from Battalion H.Qs. to find out the position of those units on our flanks, reached their positions near the railway, when they were told that there were no British troops to their front, that these positions were then the British front line..

Passing through these troops I reported to the G.O.C., 175th Inf. Bde., who directed me to LOGRE when I ascertained the position of 100th Inf. Bde., to whom I reported at about 6.30 p.m. (14th April).

The last occasion on which communication with the Companies of the Battalion was effected was at about 6 p.m. on 13th, when O.C., A Company sent a message saying that he was being heavily attacked and required ammunition, at the same time requesting/permission to carry out <u>then</u> the new dispositions which were to take effect at dusk.

After that every attempt to gain touch failed.

A runner who was sent from Battalion H.Qs. at about 7 p.m. to the Brewery, the Battalion H.Qs. we had just handed over to O.C., C Company, in order to take a message to O.C., C Company, returned to say that Germans were in occupation of the Brewery.

Other runners sent forward and to the flanks, from that hour on, failed to return. Similarly no further information of any kind came from the Companies to Battalion H.Qs.

A Sergt. of the 16th K.R.R.C. reported to me on the evening of 13th at the MAIRIE at about 7 p.m. and said that he and 3 Officers and 40 O.R. had been on the right of my B Company throughout that day, but had to withdraw. He asked for orders. I instructed him to report to my O.C., C Company at the Brewery, under whose command he would then come.

This party was later seen moving along the NEUVE EGLISE - WULVERGHEM RD. in the neighbourhood of LA TROMPE CBT. From this it would seem probable that on approaching the Brewery they found this latter place in the hands of the Germans.

Whilst in the MAIRIE there were some 20 - 30 casualties amongst the defenders, all with the exception of 3 as already stated, were evacuated.

During the operations in NEUVE EGLISE and those subsequently at Hill 70 (N.E. BAILLEUL) the following points were prominent.

(1)/

(1)   The enemy preceded his attacks by sending forward small parties under specially selected senior N.C.O's who showed the greatest leadership and bravery. Accompanied by M.G's these parties siezed the earlies opportunity of penetrating into our position and then establishing their M.G's - thus to some extent securing their ground - these advanced parties paved the way for further numbers who followed up close behind with more M.G's and Trench Mortars, these latter weapons engaged our points which offered a special resistance to their advance.

(2)   The rapidity and precision with which the enemy located all prominent features in our positions, and on to these prominent features, vigorous M.G. fire was instantly directed.

(3)   Enemy artillery appeared to work in closest liaison with the infantry, even firing at point blank range.

(4)   The use made of enemy aeroplanes to locate our advanced patrols, by dropping coloured lights, whereupon enemy artillery opened fire.

(5)   During daylight the time was employed by the enemy in dribbling forward men in very small and irregular numbers, to a position of assembly, from which, when dusk came on, attacks in strength and regular formations were launched.

(6)   Very lights were extensively employed at night by the enemy, either to.-
　(i)   Direct his columns in rear, or
　(ii)   to give the line for his artillery, or
　(iii) to signal his progress.

(7)   Where our posts were placed in the open or in front of hedges these positions were very quickly discovered by the enemy and consequently soon became the targets for his guns.
　　Had they been placed close behind hedges, they would have been screened both from view of the enemy observers and scouts and also from his aeroplanes, whilst at the same time would have been afforded the protection against being rushed and fire being directed through the hedges. Moreover, concealed communication to and from these posts would have been maintained, whereas communication in most cases, sooner or later became almost impossible when exposed to view of the enemy.

(8)   The urgent need for infantry being supported with trench mortars and Stokes gunners was demonstrated both in the MAIRIE and at Hill 70. At the latter place when the enemy gained a footing in the wood about 300 yards in front of our posts, L.G's and M.G's failed to dislodge him, our artillery failed to get the range to this wood and direct infantry assaults, though attempted met with little success, besides being too costly. T.M's or Stokes guns could have, it is certain, made the enemy's position in this wood untenable.

(9)   In the absence of aeroplane observation by our artillery, F.O.O's are imperative, and in their connections either communication by means of 'phone or visual must be maintained. Should this be impossible some kind of signal to show artillery whether they are shelling short or over could be used.

(10)/

(10)   We suffered a great number of casualties from our own shells falling short, this was particularly regrettable for our own barrage came down with such intensity on our posts that it appeared that these posts were included in the S.O.S. line.

(11)   From the point of view of a Battalion Commander in the line I would like to suggest that all M.G's and Stokes guns, Trench Mortars,etc., be placed under his command in so far as their position is concerned, for in the light of recent events, when the subordinate Officer Commanding these smaller units became a casualty, the N.C.O. remaining in charge invariably came to me for instructions, which I forthwith issued, and it seems reasonable to say that the Battalion Commander has a clearer picture of the situation than these above referred to units.

(12)   As regards posts.   Instead of the system of having a few large posts, it might be suggested that smaller and more numerous posts could be employed with advantage. Knowing the rapidity with which the enemy locates our posts and then turns the attention of his trench mortars and artillery on to these posts it would perhaps be advisable to dig these smaller posts and employ a few men (6 - 8) to garrison them, with alternative small posts in front, so that in the event of any one post becoming untenable there would be another one to go forward to, and at the same time should any posts be hit by a direct shell then the loss would be essentially small.
        That very dangerous and disastrous tendency to fall back, by the survivors of posts which have become untenable by reason of direct hits by shell fire, would then be provided against if there were alternative short lengths of trench close at hand.
        The most terribly shaken soldier will readily jump into the nearest trench that gives even small cover, but in the absence of any such cover, he goes back.

(13)   On these occasions when the enemy obtained a footing in our positions, by means of an immediate counter-attack he was invariably ejected, having obtained a footing he must not be given time to secure that footing, but be attacked whilst he is still 'getting his breath' and before he can get his M.G's into position.

(14)   In spite of the generous provision of Lewis Guns per Company, application had to be made during the above described operations for more to replace those lost.
        The supply of S.A.A. was abundant, although heavy demands were made by M.G.Corps units at Hill 70.

(15)   Throughout the operations in NEUVE EGLISE, on no occasion did those units on either flank inform me of their intention to withdraw, the result being my total ignorance of their movements though I made frequent efforts to keep in touch with them.

                          (Sgd) G.J.L.STONEY, Major,
                          2nd Worcestershire Regiment.

Sources

The Imperial War Museum

The Worcestershire Regiment in the Great War (Capt. H. Fitz M Stacke MC.)

The Green Un. The Worcestershire Regiment 2nd Battalion October 1925

The Worcestershire Regiment – An Historical Note

Bisley National Shooting Centre

Ramsgate 1957 and Dover 1900 Rifle Club

London Gazette June 29th 1918. *Announcement of Lieut John James Crowe's Victoria Cross.*

Berrows Worcester Journal. Saturday July 6th 1918 and Saturday August 30th 1919.

The National Archives WO 95/2430/2 War Diary of the 2nd Battalion Worcestershire Regiment.

Salient Points Three, Tony Spagnoly and Ted Smith.

#0009 - 060718 - C0 - 229/152/6 - PB - 9781908336620